JOB INTERVIEW

THIS BOOK INCLUDES:

GUIDE TO A WINNING INTERVIEW

HOW TO ANSWER INTERVIEW QUESTIONS

JIM HUNTING

Table of Contents

BOOK 1

GUIDE TO A WINNING INTERVIEW

BOOK 2

HOW TO ANSWER INTERVIEW QUESTIONS

GUIDE TO A WINNING INTERVIEW

Questions and Answers for Job Interview Success. How to Be More Confident, Be Yourself and Answer Interview Questions.

Jim Hunting

Introduction

Whether you are a fresh college graduate or someone who is looking to kick start a new career, one of the things that you should be fully cognizant of is the dynamics of the job-hunting process including of course the often-dreaded interview portion.

While there is no right way to do an interview, there are a couple of pointers that you should take note and be mindful of to make sure that your interview goes well and hopefully helps you land your target job.

However, even before embarking on a job-hunting adventure, it is essential that you develop a deep sense of self-awareness. Knowing who you are, what your values and competencies are, as well as what your goals are will help you in coming up with a clearer vision of your future self.

Know what you do best.

Applying for a job should always be preceded by identifying the things that you are capable of doing well. A longstanding problem in the labor market is the apparent mismatch of jobs available and the skill set of the labor pool. If you want to have a job that you are competent and fully comfortable in, you should look for positions that cater to your abilities and strengths.

Find your market.

If you are looking for a job in the finance industry, it makes sense that you look for one in a financial district. If you are looking for an arts-related profession, you need to factor in the available art venues and spaces in a particular place. On some occasions, this might mean that you have to step out of your comfort zone and move in to an entirely new area.

Know how much you are worth.

Since applying for a job is essentially a way of showcasing your knowledge and experience in a particular field, then it goes without saying that you should have a clear idea of how much you should be worth. Don't be afraid to aim for the best.

Improve on your skills, if you must.

Some jobs require specialized skills, experience or educational attainment. If you are keen on earning such kind of job, then you should take the time and effort to meet the basic criteria.

Have realistic and reasonable expectations.

Your excitement and enthusiasm over the prospect of getting a job you like should be guarded by reason and logic. This doesn't mean that you should sport a pessimistic outlook, either. Basically, you should have a way of gauging your abilities and your performance in the exercise of such abilities. You should be honest enough to admit if there's any weakness you should work on or conversely, highlight the strengths that you can use as leverage in the future.

Find the right motivation.

There is nothing more powerful than being motivated to reach your goals. But motivation comes in different forms for different people. Some see money as a powerful motivating factor. In choosing jobs, they go for openings with a relatively higher pay.

Meanwhile, other people lean more toward job opportunities that provide a profound sense of satisfaction and boost their sense of self-worth. When picking jobs, these people look at the culture of the workplace and gauge it based on how being part of this particular organization can make them better.

Ideal worker mindset

But no matter the motivation, an inarguably essential factor to take into account is the importance of developing an ideal worker mindset. You must come across as a perfect fit to the job opening that you are aiming for. Your skills, attitude and character must match the requirements of this particular employment opportunity.

A good way of making yourself better prepared for the challenges of job hunting is by making yourself familiar with the dynamics of the labor market, as well as the history and background of the specific organization that you want to be a part of including the working environment.

Chapter 1: Crafting Your Cover Letter

Now that you understand what a cover letter is and its importance, it is time to learn how to craft your own well-written letter, also known as a CV.

While there are many dos and don'ts in writing a cover letter, thankfully, there is a basic pattern that every professional cover letter should follow.

You can use this guideline with your own information to ensure that your CV is always the correct format.

A basic no-fuss cover letter should consist of:

- Your Name
- Phone number
- Email address
- Date
- Addressed to the name and professional title of the hiring manager
- Name of the company you are applying for a position at

This is the most basic of cover letter guidelines, as you can see, it doesn't even contain much information on the individual. This is because while the standard guideline above is needed, the rest of the letter can be highly personalized.

Along with the above guideline, you also must add other information. This can include a variety of components, depending upon the person. Some options include:

- The address of your professional website
- Your professional title
- Your home address
- Links to your LinkedIn or Twitter
- City of Residence

While you want to illustrate your personality in your cover letter, it is important to do so in a professional manner.

For instance, you want to use an email address that illustrates professionalism. Such as [your name]@gmail.com or email@[your website].com.

You never want to include unprofessional email addresses on your cover letter or resume, as this can be a deal breaker. If your email is something such as SexyTiger135@gmail.com or CottonCandyFTW@yahoo.com you will want to create a new email address for professional purposes.

Ideally, you want to stick with either Gmail or an email created with your own website domain, as these are seen as the most professional options.

Similarly, you should avoid using an email address that contains your current work information.

If your professional email address contains your current company or position, it is disrespectful to both your previous company and the new company to use this address.

Lastly, ensure that your contact information is consistent across the board. You want your resume, cover letter, and social media to all use the same information.

You now understand the basic format of your cover letter and the most important information to include in each and every CV. However, these are only the bare bones of a cover letter.

You still need to include information that will make the employer want to hire you. For that, follow the tips below to get a customized and successful letter.

Use the Proper Format

The cover letter, while it can show your personality, needs to remain professional.

For this reason, use the same formal format that you would for any professional or business matter.

For this, you want to use either Times New Roman, Calibri, or Arial fonts in size twelve or ten point.

When writing your name, contact information, and date align them along the top of the letter. Lastly, keep the cover letter to a single page with three or four short paragraphs.

Address the Hiring Manager

Some people may address this cover letter's to "whom it may concern," but this is bad practice.

This will make it appear that you either have not done enough research on the company or that you are mass producing this CV to send out to multiple companies.

Instead, you want to directly address your letter to the person who will be hiring you. This person's name may be written in the job posting.

However, if it is not, then try calling the main phone number for the company and asking for both the name and position of the hiring manager.

This may seem like an unnecessary step; however, it will leave a big impression on the hiring manager and increase your likelihood of getting hired.

This will also give you the opportunity to learn more about the company in general.

If you have any personal connections to the company and would-be colleges then feel free to subtly mention these connections.

By doing this, it gives the hiring manager the opportunity to ask the people who know you their opinion of your work ethic and capability.

Use Keywords

Often times, employers don't simply read through every cover letter they receive. Instead, they may run it through a filtering software that is meant to scan for keywords in resumes.

This software allows an employer to wade through resumes and cover letters, only reading those that match their preferred keywords of desired skills and experience.

In order to get your cover letter read, you need to naturally and conversationally incorporate key phrases and words that fit the job's description.

You can do this by mentioning how many years of experience you have, degree type, developed skills, communication and organization abilities, and any history you have in project management.

Some examples of keywords to use include:

- Skill Keywords:

- Planned, wrote, analyzed, designed, quantified, programmed, trained, taught, surveyed, organized, critiqued, inspected, assembled, solved, engineered, maintained, operated, administered, appraised, audited, budgeted, calculated, projected, researched, directed, developed, performed, acted, established, fashioned, illustrated, founded, programmed, coached, communicated, instructed, enabled, encouraged, guided, informed, built.

- Result-Oriented Keywords:

- Implemented, planned, managed, upgraded, assessed, strengthened, persuaded, initiated, adapted, oversaw, lead, redesigned, helped, launched, began, adopted, boosted, headed, operated, increased, trained, educated, reformulated, expanded, acquired, generated, produced, initiated.

- Self-Descriptive Keywords:

- Independent, creative, unique, attentive, dependable, responsible, ambitious, analytical, sensitive, reliable, enthusiastic, adaptable, logical, initiative, efficient, experienced, effective, sincere, productive, personable, instrumental, honest, adept, loyal, diplomatic, insightful.

Keep the First Paragraph Strong

At the beginning of your letter, you should start with a strong and personal greeting directly to the hiring manager.

But, don't slack off after this greeting.

It is vital to have a strong opening paragraph that catches their attention and draws them into reading your entire letter and your resume.

This means that you absolutely must avoid any misspellings or typos.

You also need to include something interesting about yourself that sets you apart from the crowd.

While the entire cover letter is important, the most important areas to strengthen are the beginning and then end.

After all, it is vital to make a good first impression and leave off with a good impression.

Highlight Relevant Details

In your cover letter, you are able to go into more detail on how and why you are a perfect fit for a job.

While a resume simply highlights your experience, the cover letter explains why this experience makes you an ideal fit.

Therefore, when highlighting your experiences, be sure to stick with experiences and reasoning that fits the specific job.

For instance, if you were a waiter and are now applying to a job in another field, it may not at first appear that it is a relevant experience. Yet, the cover letter allows you to explain why this experience actually makes you the best fit. You can take the time to explain that your interactions with customers, managing disputes, and working as a team will enable you to better do the new job, if you are hired. If possible, try to use data and numbers to explain your strengths, as employers like to see hard numbers.

Tie Yourself to the Company

Whenever possible, speak of yourself in relation to the company.

This will show the hiring manager that you have knowledge of the company and convey enthusiasm.

You can do this by mentioning how much you care about the company's vision or mission.

If you have followed the company or used their products/services of years, you can mention how much they have beneficially impacted your life.

Similarly, you want to speak within the letter as if you have already been hired.

For instance, imagine that you are speaking to a manager after being hired and they ask why you chose the company.

You can answer with your interest in the company and enthusiasm about working for them.

For instance: "When I discovered DreamCloud Animation was hiring, I simply knew I must apply. I had been searching for a company that truly makes a difference, where I could make an impact. I was inspired by the company and their mission to consistently produce high-quality animation that tells a story to warm people hearts and increase the appreciation of the seemingly mundane. I believe in the mission of DreamCloud Animation, and I wanted to work with you so that I too can make a difference."

Name the Position Title

It may seem simple, but it is important to add in the name of the job title you are applying for.

This helps the employer to know that you are knowledgeable and understand what you are applying for.

This can be done easily, as you can say something to the effect of "Regarding the Graphic Design position," *or* "I am writing to apply for Floor Manager position [company name] recently advertised."

Illustrate How You Can Solve a Specific Problem

Are you a problem-solver? While stating this in a cover letter may seem beneficial, it actually has little impact on the hiring manager.

After all, what problems can you solve? By simply stating you are a problem-solver you might as well be saying you know how to "solve" the problem of not knowing what to eat for breakfast when the pantry is nearly bare.

Instead of telling the hiring manager that you are great at solving problems, detail exactly what problems you can help them solve.

How can you use your skills to help the company better and solve their problems? Take time to consider exactly what you can do for the company and then detail it.

Share a Story

You want your cover letter to be captivating, interesting, and informative.

One of the most successful ways in which you can do this is by sharing a story or anecdote about yourself.

This can allow the employer to get a better idea of your personality, work style, and skills. Although, it is important to share the right story while keeping it short and sweet.

How do you know if a story is right for your cover letter?

You can start by looking at the job description and researching the company.

Once you understand the position and company well, you can compare your skills, talents, and experience compared to what they are looking for in an employee.

For instance, the company might be looking for a team player, someone with communication skills, and a person who is able to resolve conflicts, and a person who is able to train those under them.

Keeping these aspects in mind, you can consider your past and think of an anecdote that contains as many of these traits as possible.

For instance, you might have volunteered at a place in which you managed a team, kept everyone on good terms while resolving conflicts, trained newcomers, and communicated the needs of the day to those working with you.

You can share this anecdote, while specifically mentioning these skills and traits you made use of.

By being able to hear a story of how you specifically have used your skills and traits in the past a company can get a better idea of how you will work on the job.

Stay Honest

The worst mistake you can make in your cover letter is being dishonest.

Not only does this have moral implications, but it will also come back to bite you.

If you tell the company that you have an experience, talent, or skill that you don't actually have, then they will find out in the future.

They will soon learn that you are unable to do what you stated, and it will get you into trouble.

Instead, stay honest while putting your best foot forward and highlighting your actual skills and traits in the most positive light possible.

Be You, Stay Unique

The cover letter is created to set you apart from the crowd, which your resume alone is unable to do.

Yet, many people fail to capture any of their unique qualities into their CV, leaving the hiring manager unimpressed and on their way to the next candidate.

This all too often happens when a person uses phrases such as "Hello, I am John/Jane Smith. I am a hard-working, multi-tasking, and detail-oriented person. I was born to be a leader and believe I could help your company."

A hiring manager or employer isn't going to be interested in a basic cover letter template that sounds as if it could be created by anyone. Highlight how you are unique and stand out from the crowd.

You can do this by switching out common words. For instance, instead of saying you are a *natural-born leader*" you might say "*I excel when leading a team.*"

This helps your cover letter to sound different, catching a person's eye better.

However, the best way you can stay unique is to share your stories and personality.

Work these into the letter by sharing with the hiring manager stories and examples of how you can best help the company, excel in the position, and make use of your strengths.

Illustrate Your Goals, Passions, and Dreams

An employer doesn't only want to know your strengths and why you are qualified for a position, they also want to know why you care and the career path you envision.

After all, they know that the more passionate a person is about their work the more motivated they are to do a job well done.

If you are passionate about the career, express this. If you dream about becoming a manager and leading a team, let them know.

If your goal is to advance in your field, don't hesitate to add that.

An example: "Graphic design and integrating it into advertisements has been my passion for many years, which is why I pursued my degree in graphic design at New York University. Not only do I dream of working in this field, but I believe my skills will help me to excel. My enthusiasm, passion, and work ethic will push me forward to new heights, making me a wonderful candidate for the position of Graphic Designer at Think! Advertisements."

End on a High Note

When concluding your cover letter in the last paragraph, be sure to use one or two sentences to reiterate why you are the perfect candidate for the job.

As most people will read the resume directly after the cover letter, you want to use this final paragraph to highlight anything important that you want the manager to notice following in your resume.

After you have reiterated anything important, you want to mention that you have attached your resume and that you are looking forward to hearing back from them.

You might even give them a date by which you will contact them if you don't hear back.

For instance: "Thank you for taking the time to consider me for the position of Graphic Designer. I hope my resume, which I have included, proves to be helpful. I look forward to hearing back from you in the near future. I will stay in touch, making a phone call in one week, unless I hear back from you in the meantime."

Unique Visual Format

Humans naturally remember something when it stands out from the crowd. For this reason, instead of simply typing out and printing your cover letter, it is a good idea to give it a unique visual format.

However, this must be done carefully. You don't want to use bright and flashy gimmicks that will turn off the reader or make it more difficult to focus on the contents of the letter. This means that you want to avoid brightly colored paper, unusual fonts, more than two types of fonts, or colored fonts for the letter contents.

The cover letter must remain professional and easy to read.

If you do choose to play around with the visual format, look at some of our examples below to get an idea of what works.

While you want the body text of the letter to use black ink, you might decide to use a dark blue or green ink for the heading text.

Adding a picture of yourself doesn't hurt, as long as it doesn't take up too much of the page space.

Try to arrange your text on the page so that it is visually appealing, rather than appearing in one big difficult to read block.

While you shouldn't use brightly colored paper, you can use a high-quality white or off-white paper.

Chapter 2: Sell yourself like a pro

The job market today is more competitive than ever. Think of it this way:

It's easy to advertise a product when there are fewer competitors. All you need to do is to show the product to the consumer (example: show potential consumers an image of a bath soap and they'll buy it because they know what it's for.) However, if there are several similar products on the market, showing the consumers an image of the product is not enough to convince consumers to buy it. You have to remind them what it's for, how it will make their lives easier/better, and all the other reasons why they should buy it (this is when you start using commercial models, the perfect script, perfect background music, perfect packaging, etc.) More importantly, you have to show potential consumers why your product is better than all the others. It's for this reason why TV and printed ads strive to be more colorful, more interesting, and more unique.

And with the number of job-seekers out there, this is exactly how you should sell yourself as well.

What makes a great salesman great? It's when he's able to take control of the situation while making the clients believe that they're the ones in control. An experienced salesman will discuss the needs and concerns of the clients while persuading the customers that what he's selling is the answer to their problems.

A job interview is no different. View the interview as an opportunity to make a sale. You take control and then subtly guide the interviewer into making you a job offer. Your main goal during the interview is to transform yourself in the eyes of the interviewer from a total stranger to someone that his company must buy.

Listen actively

One of the greatest misconceptions about interviews is that it is the interviewee's moment in the spotlight where he can speak as much as he wants to about himself. On the contrary, active listening is twice as important as speaking in interviews. While a chatty candidate's enthusiasm to please the employer may seem amusing, it doesn't always result to a productive interview. Simply put, it's not about how much you say but how much value your words contain.

Listen closely to what the interviewer says about his business/organization. Your responses must be based according to his company's needs. This way, you turn from being a job applicant to a partner who's eager to share ideas and solutions.

Be on the lookout for conversation builders
From time to time, the interviewer will say some things that you can use to build an interesting conversation.

Example:

Interviewer: "The low inventory turnover is one of our biggest problems."

Applicant: "I understand completely. I've had experience in finding solutions for low inventory turnover in my previous position. Exactly what type of problems are you facing at the moment?"

Mirror
When you listen, don't just sit there like a cold marble statue. This would embarrass or offend your interviewer. Worse, it might send the message that you're not that interested in the job after all.

Respond through your body language. Nod in agreement from time to time. That said, don't exaggerate your responses by agreeing to every single thing that the interviewer says. You must have your own opinions. Even so, restrain yourself and put your opinions on hold long enough to hear the interviewer out. You may not 100% agree with what the interviewer is saying, but play your cards right by finding a common ground and taking it from there.

Example:

Interviewer: "I think _____ is highly important. To accomplish this, we must use Approach A or Approach C."

Applicant: "I certainly agree that _____ is of primary importance. And I also favor approach C. While I can see the advantages of using Approach A, have you considered trying Approach B?"

Interviewer: "Why?"

Applicant: "Well, based from my experience, one of the greatest advantages of Approach B is..."

Lean forward slightly or sit at the edge of your seat to communicate to the interviewer that you find the exchange stimulating. Practice the art of mirroring the interviewer's message. This means that you match his/her tone. When he's excited about something, reflect his enthusiasm. When he adopts a serious tone while discussing a certain topic, reflect his seriousness.

Important: Limit your use of mirroring techniques, especially when it comes to mimicking your interviewer's body language.

It's true that mimicry may serve as a social glue that can assist in the promotion of rapport between human beings. In fact, years of research has proved that generally, subtly mirroring another person's tone, vocabulary, words, posture, and gestures can make you seem more likable to that individual. However, more than one recent study by psychological researchers reveal that when it comes to job interviews, mimicry must be kept to a minimum, especially when there is more than one interviewer.

In an experiment done by scientists from University of California, San Diego, several mock interviews were recorded. In the interviews, some of the participants mimicked the interviewers' gestures while others did not. After this, the scientists asked judges to watch the videos and measure the interviewees' level of competence, likeability, and credibility. The result? The judges found the candidates who kept mirroring to a minimum to be more competent, credible, and likeable.

A similar study was conducted by a team of experts at Texas Tech and Drew Universities. According to the study, mirroring can have negative effects on an applicant's success. This is because humans mimic not only positive gestures but also negative gestures as well. In other words, if your interviewer happens to find you less likeable or if he's just having a bad day, mirroring his gestures, his facial expression, or his tone of voice will only cause you to send a negative message to his subconscious. You become a living mirror of his negative emotions. Seeing you reflect how he's feeling inside will only serve to reinforce his negative perception of you.

Therefore, use mirroring strategies sparingly. Instead, concentrate on using body language to convey confidence and enthusiasm. You already have a lot on your mind during an interview and this is one less thing that you should worry about.

Repeat and rephrase

Rephrasing is one way to prove to the interviewer that you've been listening to him attentively. Like mirroring, rephrasing must be kept to a minimum. Make sure you restate only the most important points to the interviewer.

Example:

"If I understand you correctly..."
"From what I understand, you're saying that..."

Remind the interviewer why you're there in the first place

This may seem a bit frustrating, but in case the interviewer comes unprepared, his rambling thoughts may lead the conversation into an unpredictable path that will hinder you from selling yourself most effectively. At this point, your job is to give him a little nudge back to the right direction.

Example: "I just can't tell you how excited I am to be here. I believe that what I have to offer could be of use to this company."

With a statement like this, you're placing the focus back on the reasons why you're the right person for the job.

You might come across an interviewer who likes to monopolize the conversation. Should you butt in? Definitely. How else would you be able to have the opportunity to sell yourself?

But how do you interrupt a talkative interviewer's monologue without seeming rude?

First, absorb what you can from the interviewer's words. What you're actually listening in for are conversation builders and opportunities to highlight your selling points. Once it comes out of your interviewer's non-stop mouth, pounce on it.

Example:

INTERVIEWER: "As I was saying, one of the biggest challenges in this business is to guarantee sufficient cash flow--"

APPLICANT: "Allow me to interrupt you for a second. What you're saying is just too interesting. Management of cash flow is actually one of my main areas of interest. I have a couple of fresh ideas which you might be interested in hearing and I can't wait to hear your thoughts on them..."

Another type of interviewer you might come across is the stressed out, overworked type. He/she may be distracted during the whole interview. He/she may even cut you short to answer phone calls. Instead of feeling indignant, express your sympathy. Then, use it as a way to bring up the value that you can add to the company.

Example:

"Wow, you really are very busy during this time of the year. I know what it's like and I can totally see why the company could use someone with my skills and experience."

This will direct the interviewer's attention back to you.

Remember: There are times when the job interviewing task falls on a chiefly technical person. When this happens, you get an interviewer who will lead the conversation into a discussion of technical matters. While it's important to demonstrate your technical know-how, it is also necessary to remember that this isn't all that your interviewer wants to know about you. Naturally, he'll also want to know what you would be like as an employee. Chances are, he may be having a hard time communicating what he really wants to ask you. The solution? Look for a way to connect your technical skills with your transferrable skills. Provide examples of situations where you used *both*.

Keep in mind the lessons that your high school teacher taught you

Whoever said that high school subjects have no practical application in real life wasn't familiar with the rules of successful interviews. Remember when your grammar school teacher kept hounding you about using a substantial topic sentence, an engaging introduction, and a powerful conclusion in your essays? Well, you have to follow the same rules when answering interview questions.

Open with your topic sentence. Then, proceed with statements that support the topic sentence. Finally, end with a conclusion that summarizes your point.

Example:

"I understand that it's my job to find out and cater to our potential clients' needs, which will, in turn, enable me to INCREASE *the company's sales*. This is why I made it my business to help the company to earn _____ dollars in sales last quarter. I was able to *persuade* former clienteles such as _____ and _____ to *purchase* the company's most recent products. I also *secured* new clients such as _____ and _____.

Moreover, I *collaborated* with _____ and _____ departments to help draw more attention to the company's flagship product, which is _____, and thus, maximizing its visibility to potential consumers. *Within one year of being in the company, I increased the company's sales by _____ % through diligence, social skills, salesmanship abilities, and by being a team player."*

Phrases that Keep the Ball Rolling

Using the following magic phrases will aid in maintaining the momentum of the conversation:

"I agree..."

"I can certainly relate..."

"That's interesting..."

"We should talk about..."

"Tell me more..."

"We should pursue that further..."

"That's also one of my biggest concerns..."

There are also phrases that could stop a conversation dead in its tracks. Here are a few examples of what you must avoid:

"Definitely not..."

"I absolutely disagree..."

"There is no way..."

"It's impossible…"

"It's final…"

"That's not how it should be done…"

Be on the lookout for 'Buy Signals'
You'll know an interviewer is interested in you when he starts using phrases such as the following:

"Sounds great."

"Interesting."

"I like that!"

Buy signals like these are signs that you've successfully caught your employer with your hook. Now it's time for you to reel him in, proverbially speaking. You do this by expounding on the idea that captured his interest. That said, unless they're really, really impressed, interviewers are rarely expressive. Often, their buy signals come in the form of a request for you to elaborate further on the topic.

Example:

"Can you tell me more about…"

"I'd like to hear more about…"

"Let's go back to…"

"Would you care to be more specific about…"

Now, most interviewees would dread the idea of being asked to speak more about a certain topic. Since you're reading this book, you shouldn't be feeling this way any longer! This is an indicator that you've hit the right button. But what is the correct way of expounding on an idea?

In marketing, a product's *features* refer to the characteristics of the product (ex: portable, compact, etc.) If you're a product, then your features are your skills (ex: great managerial skills, reliable, trustworthy, etc.) On the other hand, a product's *benefits* refer to the positive things that it can do for the user (ex: portable, compact materials can be used while on the go and are easy to store.)

It's your *features* that will catch the interviewer's attention. To draw him in, you now have to present your *benefits*. In other words: *How can your skills make the employer's business/life more profitable/better?*

Example:

"I believe that the most important part of my position as an assistant manager is to *provide you* with more *time* to pursue higher responsibilities. My goal is to support you in the management of the store so you can have more valuable time in your hands."

Make a closing statement that closes the sale
You're playing the part of a salesman. This means you're not leaving the interview room without urging the employer to seal the deal.

Wrong: "So, did I get the job?"/"Did I do okay?"
This comes across as overly presumptuous, pathetic, and perhaps worst of all, needy. You're likely to end up with the standard dismissive response: "Don't call us. We'll call you."

Correct:

"Based on all that I've told you, don't you think I would be a great fit for the company?"
This part can be quite tricky. You need to make use of a closing statement that will actually extract a positive answer from the employer. To use or not to use closing statements like this will depend on how well you've established rapport with your interviewer and how effectively you were able to answer the interview questions. If you have a good feeling about the interview, proceed to prompt the employer into action. If not, follow a different route:

"Thank you so much for your time, Mr./Mrs./Ms. _____. It has been great pleasure and I do believe I have a great deal to offer to this institution. But please, if there's anything that I wasn't able to discuss to your satisfaction, do let me know. What could I tell you to encourage you to make a proposal?"

Keep in mind that it's not about pressuring the employer to make a decision on the spot. This is about increasing your chances of urging the employer to commit to you positively. Closing statements like these suggest a hint of urgency without the sense of impatience or desperation. It simply reminds the interviewer of your value.

Chapter 3: Experience Related Questions

What would your boss say is an area you could improve on?

Question Type:

Background and Personality

Question Analysis:

The interviewer will use this question to assess how well the candidate embraces critical feedback. No matter how strong a performance review might be, most managers will offer up at least one area for improvement. The interviewer is looking for the candidate to be candid about an area for improvement and discuss how they are taking action. Ideally, your response would discuss an area you are new to and investing time to improve.

What to Avoid:

You should avoid criticizing your boss's judgement. A response such as "my boss told me I need to pay better attention to detail but I disagree with her assessment" will not go over well with the interviewer. It will portray you as someone who is not receptive to critical feedback from superiors. You should also avoid saying something such as "my boss has never suggested an area for improvement." Remember that this question is a hypothetical. If your boss has not provided critical feedback, then you can still come up with your own area for self-improvement. Finally, you should avoid discussing areas that would be concerning to the interviewer. If you are interviewing for a sales position and you mention that you need to become better at communicating with customers, you will create a cause for concern.

Example Response:

My boss would say I could get better at recognizing when my work load is at full capacity and delegating work. I recently moved into a supervisor role, but I still put too much on my own plate which causes me unnecessary stress. When tasks and projects come up I tend to gravitate toward taking full ownership over them instead of working with my team to find out who is in the best position to do the work.

I recently implemented weekly update meetings with my team so that we can run through everyone's workload and availability. These meetings have helped me identify opportunities to delegate project work throughout our team to create a better balance for everyone.

Why is there a gap in your employment history? (if applicable)

Question Type:

Background and Personality

Question Analysis:

If the interviewer asks this question they are looking for an upfront and honest response. The best way to approach this question largely depends on the reason for the gap. If you were laid off, you should provide some details of the situation and discuss why the company decided to reduce headcount. If you took a leave of absence, you can explain the situation from a high level but there is no need to go into too many personal details. For example, "I had a health scare I needed to resolve" or "a family member became ill and needed my full attention" is enough detail. You should try to incorporate positive items in your employment history before and after the gap. It is also beneficial if you can discuss your ambitious intentions during the gap period.

What to Avoid:

You should avoid getting defensive with your response. Your answer should not be centered around any excuses with past employment. Whether it was a result of a prior job or a personal reason that resulted in the gap, you should avoid going into too many unnecessary details.

Example Response:

When I previously worked at XYZ Company, they unexpectedly lost their largest customer and needed to take drastic action to stay in business. 25% of the sales force was laid off including most members on my team. It felt like a punch in the gut, but I understood the Company did not have much of a choice.

As I considered my next steps, I decided that it was important not to jump at the first opportunity but instead take the time to find the right fit for my career. I treated the job search like a full-time position, spending most of my days making new connections and setting up coffee or lunch meetings with business contacts in the area. I also made time to take a two-week online sales training course I had been interested in for over a year. After 4 months of networking and consideration, I decided to accept a position for a territory sales manager at XYZ Company.

What are three skills all professionals in this field should possess?

Question Type:

Industry and Company Specific

Question Analysis:

The interviewer will likely ask this question using the name of the profession such as "What are three skills all accountants should possess?" You should be prepared to discuss skills that are highly relevant to your profession and align closely with the job description. The interviewer is typically looking for the candidate to hone in on certain skill sets that are a must for the profession (i.e. excellent verbal communication skills for a nurse). The following skills are highly relevant to nearly all professions:

Effective communicator, attention to detail, excellent planner, and strong time management.

What to Avoid:

Your answer should avoid overly generic skills that are presumed for all professionals such as "hard worker." Your answer should also not be a laundry list of skills. Be sure to discuss how each skill benefits the professional in their respective field.

Example Response:

(Example response is for accountants)

Successful accountants focus on attention to detail to ensure their work is complete and accurate. We work in a profession where small mistakes can have profound consequences. Attention to detail in this profession means fully understanding the scope of the work and expectations before completing it. It also means critical self-reviews before finalizing our work.

Accountants should also be excellent at planning their work at a micro and macro level. Time management is essential to staying on track and meeting deadlines.

Finally, all successful accountants should be effective communicators. Whether it is meeting with a boss, collaborating with team members, or discussing an issue with a client, accountants need to have strong written and verbal communication skills.

What was something you did not like about your previous (or current) position?

Question Type:

Background and Personality

Question Analysis:

This can be a tricky question because candidates are often tempted to heavily criticize their previous job or employer, but this can reflect poorly on the candidate's own personality and professionalism. You should discuss why you did not prefer a certain management style, a team dynamic, or a job limitation from a professional perspective.

What to Avoid:

Unless something drastic happened (such as fraud or harassment), it is important to stay away from character attacks or interoffice drama because the interviewer may associate it with your own personality. It is also wise to avoid criticism of common challenges that occur in most work environments such as "too much stress," "long hours," or "a demanding boss." These answers may lead to the interviewer questioning whether the candidate can handle adversity which will come up often in most positions.

Example Response:

Overall, I was really satisfied with my previous position. I worked with a great team and grew as a professional. I do wish I would have had more leadership opportunities in my previous role. The company was traditional in the sense that most project work was initiated and micro managed by the company's leadership. I thrive in an environment that offers leadership opportunities for all employees.

Question Type:

Behavioral

Question Analysis:

The interviewer will use this question to assess the candidate's team working capabilities. They want to know that the candidate possesses sufficient emotional intelligence to successfully adapt to the various personalities of co-workers. You should discuss an example that shows your ability to effectively communicate with a differing personality to achieve the desired results.

What to Avoid:

You should avoid criticizing a team member's personality. You should also avoid examples of working around another team member or excluding them from the work. The interviewer wants to see that you are able to adapt to various situations to find positive ways to work together with other team members.

Example Response:

S/T: Last year I lead a system implementation project with four other team members. I scheduled weekly update meetings to discuss the status of the project and to encourage collaboration on technical issues we were encountering. I noticed that one of our team members was extremely quiet during our team meetings, but he would often email me afterwards with excellent insight and ideas about the issues we had just discussed in the team setting.

Not hearing his ideas until after our meetings was hurting our team collaboration. It was also inefficient for me to communicate his ideas back to the team versus all of us discussing them during the meetings.

A: I looked into his experience and employment history and noted that he had just graduated from college and joined the company one month prior. Instead of talking with him about the issue during the next team meeting, I decided to schedule a one-on-one meeting. I explained to him that I was a bit nervous and shy when I first started with the company and that it was completely normal. I also tried to boost his confidence by explaining how valuable his follow up ideas had been toward the project. I explained the benefits of speaking up during team meetings but made sure not to make him feel too much pressure.

R: Over the course of the next few weeks we all started to observe him grow more comfortable with sharing his input during the team meetings. While he may be disposed to a more reserved personality, the ability to acknowledge that and work with him enabled us to use his talents to add more value to our team.

Do you prefer working in a team setting or independently?

Question Type:

Background and Personality

Question Analysis:

This question can be tricky to some candidates because it sounds as if the interviewer is asking them to take up a definitive preference for one setting over the other. However, most positions require candidates to work both independently and within a group. Unless the job description explicitly calls for working independently or in a team setting at all times, the best response is to explain that you are comfortable working in both environments.

What to Avoid:

It is okay if you prefer working independently over working with a team or vice versa but you should avoid making a bold preference in your answer. The interviewer may view your strong preference as a sign that you are weak in the other area.

Example Response:

It largely depends on the situation. Some projects and tasks are best accomplished through team work and collaboration while others are more effectively completed through independent work. I have a do-whatever-it-takes mindset and feel comfortable as a team player collaborating in a group setting but can also buckle down and work independently when needed.

Did you get along with your prior boss?

Question Type:

Background and Personality

Question Analysis:

The interviewer will use this question to get a better sense of the candidate's ability to work well with superiors. The interviewer wants to know whether you create or burn bridges. You will usually only hurt yourself by heavily criticizing your previous or current boss. Unless your boss did something highly unethical or illegal, you should focus on a positive answer.

What to Avoid:

You should avoid personal insults and character attacks when describing your previous boss. If your answer is strongly critical of your boss, the interviewer will likely view you as someone who does not respect superiors or get along well with co-workers.

Example Response:

I enjoyed working for my former boss. She never let her team get bored with their work. I was always presented with new challenges and learning opportunities. She also placed a strong emphasis on team communication and had an open-door policy for new ideas. Her management style helped me grow as a professional.

What type of salary are you seeking?

Question Type:

Background and Personality

Question Analysis:

Unlike question #69, you should not offer up a dollar amount in your response to this question. Instead, focus your answer on your enthusiasm for the position and desire to receive a competitive offer. Effective salary negotiators typically avoid being the first one to throw out a figure.

What to Avoid:

You should avoid discussing a specific desired salary figure in your response.

Example Response:____

I am excited about the opportunities that come with this position but have not focused on a specific salary figure. If you were to offer me the job, I would hope to get an offer that is competitive with the salary range for this position while taking into consideration my experience and skillset.

Tell me about a time you had to deal with a difficult co-worker. What was the outcome?

Question Type:

Behavioral

Question Analysis:

The interviewer will ask this question to assess the candidate's ability to manage conflict in the work setting. They want to know that the candidate will not ignite a conflict but will also not run away from it. Your answer should demonstrate that you are able to work through a disagreement in a professional manner and find resolution toward a common goal.

What to Avoid:

When discussing why a co-worker was difficult to work with you should avoid insulting them or getting into too many personal details about their character. Your answer should focus more on the resolution than the individual. You should also avoid discussing tedious or irrelevant conflicts such as "she always eats my lunch from the refrigerator."

Example Response:____

S/T: In my prior role as a financial analyst, I was tasked with testing our key financial reports when updates were made to our ERP system. After a significant update, I noted that one of our accounts receivable reports was broken. The data it produced was critical to our quarterly reporting package which was due in three days. The systems analyst who managed the technical side of the financial reports was not responsive to my emails or phone calls and when I stopped by his desk to let him know the importance of fixing the report, he blew me off.

A: I was frustrated with his response and lack of interest in helping our team get the report fixed. However, I remained calm and requested a meeting with him to sit down for fifteen minutes to help clear the air. He apologized for not being attentive to our request and explained that he had five different projects going on and was working thirteen-hour days to keep up. We both decided it was best to schedule a meeting with him and his manager to explain our team's urgent situation and help prioritize his time.

R: After meeting with his manager, she was able to shuffle around some of his project work to ensure our report was fixed on time. They were both appreciative that I took the time to sit down with them to explain the situation and find a solution that worked well for everyone.

Chapter 4: Education Questions

The more recent your graduation, the more intense the interest will be in your education. Because your work experience may be limited, expect to be quizzed for clues to your interests and motivation. For example, how you chose your college and your major (or why you switched), what your extracurricular activities were, any internships you had, and any future career plans (or why you didn't graduate or attend college). Of course, the more your college days recede into the distant past, the less interest there will be in your education. The interviewer can then focus his or her eagle eyes on your work experience.

Why did you choose your major and minor?

These courses were relevant to my chosen career and provided a solid foundation for it.

What the interviewer is asking/looking for: The interviewer wants a sense of your thinking process and interests, and this seems like a good place to start.

Good answer: Give a reasonable reason why. In many jobs, such as computer programming or engineering, it's expected that you majored in computer science or engineering. In other jobs, a wide variety of majors is found in employees. Or perhaps you are passionately interested in the subject, even if it's not "practical." Even if you majored in the Greek and Roman classics, philosophy, or Far East studies, and are interviewing for a job where this is not remotely relevant, be prepared to defend your choice without being defensive. But regardless, be ready to discuss the skills you learned, whether it's researching, writing, communication, or analytical skills.

Bad answer: An answer that shows lack of thought, laziness, or lack of direction. "Because I had to choose something," "It was cool" or "an easy A," or because your parents insisted, your friends were majoring in it, or the workload was lighter than other majors.

What extracurricular activities did you take part in?

I was on my college debate team, arguing topics from ethical to economic issues—and it was a good preparation for my business career.

What the interviewer is asking/looking for: The interviewer wants more of a sense of your interests and how you occupy your leisure time. They hope that you are a well-rounded person who devotes energy and time to something besides your studies.

Good answer: Show that you were interested and involved in things outside school hours—the more these are job-related or show traits the job requires, the better. Perhaps you worked on your college newspaper or yearbook as a prelude to your career in public relations or magazine, newspaper, or book publishing. Or your college basketball games taught you the importance of teamwork and listening to your coach. If you were busy working to pay for college or family bills, with little or no time for clubs or sports, don't be afraid to admit this, noting how you got a jump start on the work world and responsibility over your peers.

Bad answer: Anything that smacks of being a couch potato who simply watched TV or goofed off with your frat buddies after (or instead of) your classes.

Did you have an internship or a cooperative work-study program? If so, what did you learn?

My work-study program taught me a great deal about the field and valuable skills like working with others or research skills, which tie into the job I am seeking.

What the interviewer is asking/looking for: An internship (paid or unpaid) or cooperative work-study program is an excellent way to demonstrate work experience while still in college, differentiate yourself from your peers, and show seriousness of intent.

Good answer: Even if yours was of the coffee-fetching, photocopying, ho-hum variety, highlight the good points, like the chance to actually see and hear how the work was done and network with colleagues.

Bad answer: Bad-mouthing your internship or work-study program, having one in an utterly unrelated field (which makes the interviewer wonder about your real interest in this job), or acting like a smug know-it-all because of your experience.

An internship or cooperative work-study program isn't just a great way to land work experience that looks good on your resume—it may lead to a job.

Employers hired 38 percent of their interns and almost 51 percent of their work-study students, a survey of 360 employers by NACE found.

Why are you looking for a job in a field other than in your major?

I enjoyed a volunteer work in this field so much I wanted to switch.

What the interviewer is asking/looking for: The interviewer wants to know your thinking behind your change of direction. Changes of direction are common among young job-seekers—and many older ones as well—but he or she wants to be convinced this job in this field is right for you, now.

Good answer: Make a case on how you looked more carefully at your career goals and the job you are interviewing for is more suitable for various reasons. Perhaps it's a fast-growing field with more opportunity - and jobs for medieval French literature majors were limited. Focus squarely on this job, and relate the skills you developed in your major and any work experience to it as much as possible.

Bad answer: A vague response that reveals you haven't given much thought to your change of direction, and perhaps are taking a scattershot approach to your career planning.

Name an accomplishment during your college years that you are proud of...

I captained the debate team and led it to victory.

What the interviewer is asking/looking for: The interviewer is looking for evidence that you devoted time and energy to setting a positive goal and achieving it, and demonstrated traits or skills which hopefully you will carry over to your career.

Good answer: Anything from an extracurricular activity (at college or outside of college) to a job or volunteer work that shows traits or skills in demand in the work world, such as leadership, initiative, or communication skills. Perhaps you started a campus business making T-shirts, sponsored a child overseas with your parents, or were a candy striper at the local hospital.

Bad answer: Stunned silence, a fumbled response, or anything that tempts the interviewer to think your college years were one long spring break (or that the movie Animal House was modeled after your college experience).

Be sure to dress appropriately and act professionally during the interview, even if the company has lots of young, casually dressed employees. Young job-seekers often are casually dressed in T-shirts, flip-flops, and shorts; answer their cell phones; and pepper interviews with words like "cool," "awesome," "you know," and "like," hiring managers complain.

If you had it to do over, what college courses would you take?

Marketing and public speaking.

What the interviewer is asking/looking for: The interviewer hopes your answer will show your understanding of what the job will require, and include a relevant course or two.

Good answer: Naming courses relevant to the job at hand, in terms of knowledge or skills. For example, marketing, statistics, journalism, or public speaking courses are good answers, if you can make a case the job requires this subject matter or skills.

Bad answer: Anything that shows a complete change of direction from the major you chose, or courses irrelevant to the job at hand, like Chinese art history or philosophy.

Why did you choose your college?

Because it offered a particularly strong program in my field of interest.

What the interviewer is asking/looking for: He or she wants to see anything that shows seriousness of purpose and solid decision-malting ability.

Good answer: Perhaps your school features outstanding professors with time for their students.

Bad answer: Anything that confirms the interviewer's worst fears that you chose your school for the chance to party nonstop without your parents around, because it was the only school that accepted you, or you were forced into it because your father or mother went there.

How do you keep learning? (Or: How do you stay informed?)

I read a local newspaper and at least one business publication, such as The New York Times every day.

What the interviewer is asking/looking for: The interviewer wants to know if you are a professional with an inquiring, curious mind who strives to keep up with information and update your skills. Continuing education has never been more important than today, since technology and globalization have changed every industry.

Good answer: You regularly read trade publications in your field to keep on top of what's happening in your industry. Perhaps you also belong to a professional association, attend its conferences, meetings, or workshops and read its newsletter, take a class to learn a new skill or even a graduate degree like an MBA at night, or teach a class or speak at conferences in your field.

Bad answer: Anything that implies you stopped learning when you finished school, perhaps have not cracked a book open since then, have closed your mind to new things, and get all your information from TV.

Why didn't you finish college? (Or: Why didn't you go to college?)

I had to drop out due to lack of money but I'm willing to finish it within a few years.

What the interviewer is asking/looking for: The interviewer hopes you had a solid reason, as opposed to lack of interest in learning or discipline.

Good answer: If there was any extenuating circumstance, like needing to support your family, or health problems, by all means say so. If you are currently completing your college degree, or plan to, admit it, since this shows you realize its importance. Many people who didn't finish college, stopped after a while, or didn't attend right after high school go later in life when the timing is better, and sometimes go on to earn graduate degrees, including law and medicine.

Bad answer: An answer that shows insufficient interest in learning, displays the inability to focus or discipline yourself for very long, or leads the interviewer to wonder if you knew why then or even now.

Why did you leave college and return later?

I chose to work full-time for a while to gain solid work experience and money to complete my degree.

What the interviewer is asking/looking for: The interviewer hopes to hear any good explanation for your stop-out.

Good answer: Perhaps you traveled, which you found an invaluable learning experience, devoted time to caring for your family, or simply needed to explore your interests and focus your goals more clearly.

Bad answer: You can't articulate a reason for either why you left or why you returned, or say you simply wanted to party a lot.

Summary

You've learned your college days can reveal a lot about you, so treat them as you would your work experience. Be ready to give examples of how you demonstrated communication skills, leadership, a strong work ethic, and other things that employers value highly. Don't be surprised if your employer wants to know how you keep learning, even now.

• Tie in subjects you studied, your accomplishments, and extracurricular activities to the job at hand as much as you can.

• Talk about what you learned from internships and part-time, summer, and work-study jobs.

• Dress, speak, and act professionally in the interview.

• Give a good reason for bad grades or leaving/ not attending college, if that's the case.

Chapter 5: What You Will Bring to The Position

Once they have gotten what a sense of your personality is like, they will then start to try and investigate why they should pick you over all the other candidates. You made it past the point of being a qualified person on an individual level through your own character and experiences. This is your chance to shine and set yourself apart from all other candidates.

Remember to not simply memorize the answers that we are giving you. This only makes it harder on you in the actual interview. The point of the example answer is just so you can get a sense of a realistic and solid response. Keep it personalized to you, because setting yourself apart from the rest is of utmost importance!

"Tell me where you see yourself in the future (six months/five years/ten years from now)."

This is a common question that interviewers might even ask right at the beginning of the interview. This is a question that will be inclusive of all aspects of your life. Where do you see yourself in your career? What about your family life? In your personal goals? They don't just want to hear, "Hopefully working here!" They want to know that you are thinking about your future and that you have a plan. They want to see if they will fit into your plan. You might consider saying something like this when that question is asked:

"In six months, I hope that I am settled into a position and in a place where I can focus on really improving my skills. At the same time, I want to ensure that I'm doing my best to also consistently check in with my personal goals. Eventually, I hope to achieve a position of employment where I'm making a comfortable amount of money. I know the future is always changing so I'm also excited to see what surprises the future might bring me!"

"Why should we hire YOU?"

Every job will have several people applying for the position. All of the questions asked so far likely helped them to realize whether or not they want to hire you based on your experience and so on, but other candidates have probably fit the criteria they have too. Why should they hire you and not someone else? What stands out about you that will make you the best candidate? This is going to be specific to you. Perhaps you have a valuable skill that's hard to come by. Maybe it's something in your history that makes you unique. What are the qualities that really set you apart from the competition?

"I believe I'm the right pick because of my set of skills and experiences that I have had. I not only do what I'm asked, but I make sure to go above and beyond and deliver something greater than what I was asked. I take pride in my work, even if it is not a task I am particularly passionate about at the moment. I will always deliver work with exceptional detail and attention to the things that matter the most."

"What about this position makes you want to work here? Why do you want to get hired?"

The "Why do you want to work here" question is always going to be in the interview. It's not a trick question! Your interviewer will legitimately want to know why it is that you chose them. The obvious answer is, "Because I need a job and I saw you were hiring. I want money." This is usually the first thing that we will consider when applying to a job. While this might be the truth, try to honestly remember why it is that you want this position and not another. Have your reason prepared before even making your way into the interview. When you can give substantial answers based directly on their mission statement, then that will give you a big advantage.

"I want to work here because I have always been a lifelong supporter of this company. I have frequented the stores and I understand what the clientele is like. Not only do I think this will help me to be more passionate and dedicated to my work, but I think it helps because I will be more knowledgeable about what the business actually stands for. When I have this connection to the workplace, it is easier to go above and beyond because I have the confidence to know what my talents are and how the company will benefit from them."

"What do you know about us? How would you describe our company?"

This is a question that will require a lot of research! Make sure you Google your company before the interview. Don't just go to their site either. Read reviews if it is a service-based place or a retail location. If it is a huge company, look up news articles that might focus on them. Go on forums and see if anyone else has worked there and what their stories are like. The more you know about them, the easier this will be. Make sure that you list out what their services are, what their employees do, and what their mission statement is. This is a specific question, so make sure that your answer is based specifically on the company that you are interviewing for!

"What unique skills do you have that only apply to this specific position?"

This is another specific one that will apply only to the position that you are interviewing for. If you are looking to get hired as a front desk clerk, then you would want skills involving talking to people, handling requests, taking messages, making appointments, and other clerical work. If you are applying to be a construction worker, then you'll need to make sure that you can lift heavy things, operate heavy machinery, and have basic construction knowledge.

Whenever you are applying for a job, they'll usually have a list of objectives in their job description. Make sure that you study these. They will give you the exact insight needed to understand what unique skills that you have specifically for this job. They might have a job description that says things like:

Must be proficient in Word

Have excellent communication skills

Punctual and reliable

And so on.

Remember them, and when you get to your interview, you will be able to state them in your own way. Discuss your technical skills on the computer. Talk about how you can communicate. Give examples of how you are reliable. When you bring up keywords that they're looking for, they're going to be more likely to keep you in the back of their mind when making the final decision.

"What are you hoping to accomplish in this position?"

This is a seemingly obvious question, but it can actually catch a lot of people off guard. It seems to be one of the most obvious questions that can actually reveal a deeper truth about someone who might be applying for the job. There are a few ways that you can answer this. You can discuss how you would like to move up to a higher position if that is something you believe to be an option. Alternatively, you can discuss how you hope to gain valuable skills if it is not a position that offers a lot of growth.

"I hope while I'm working here, if hired, of course, that I can discover new skills that I may have and improve on things I need to work on while also helping the business thrive. I know the things that I need to improve on, and I have goals for myself. I think this company's goals and the goals I have for myself line up well together so that we can both mutually benefit from what I might experience here."

"How many responsibilities do you feel comfortable having at a time?"

This is a good question to help them to determine whether or not you are a multi-tasker. Some people are comfortable handling just one thing at a time, while others can handle several different things at once. Do your best to answer honestly because even if you struggle to do several things at once, that doesn't mean you're not a good employee! We all have a different pace for completing tasks so ensure that you are being honest with them. Can you handle several projects, or are you someone that works at a slower pace on one thing at a time? While you can easily lie and say that you can take on a bunch of things at once, you are just setting yourself up to make things more challenging later on. Be honest!

"I am pretty good with time management, so I don't mind taking on a few things at once. I will always try to complete tasks much faster than I say I will so that I can go above and beyond. I don't take on too much at once because I know my limits and do my best to avoid feeling overwhelmed or burnt out."

"Can you adjust quickly to a rapidly changing environment? Would you be able to change your plans if something unexpected happened?"

There may be a time when your employer has to send you to a different location, or perhaps they need you to work in a different department, depending on your skills and the versatility of management. It is up to you, then, to make sure that you know how to adapt should a situation like this occur. Be honest with them and let them know if you are going to be able to quickly adapt to situations like this if that's what you have to do later on.

"I have no problem trying new things. I appreciate having a set schedule so that I know what needs to be done, but when things change, it can just make work feel more exciting, making going to work more enjoyable. I'm not concerned about my abilities to adapt should there be a situation when I need to quickly adjust to change."

"What strong organizational skills do you have?"

Being organized is incredibly important. They can simply ask, do you have this skill, or this skill, or this skill, and so on, but instead, they are leaving this question for you to fill in the blanks. Rather than blatantly stating that you are detail oriented, punctual, and so on, put an emphasis on sharing your actual steps to become organized so that they can have a better sense of whether or not you are really someone with a great set of organization skills.

"I think organization is incredibly important in order to avoid any issues that might arise during any given project. To get organized, I first make a list of all the tasks that I need to do. From there, I will prioritize them by importance and separate them by how much time they will take and look at ways that I might be able to complete two tasks simultaneously. From there, I do my best to adhere to timelines, always giving myself a little extra time to account for any incidents that might occur!"

"If you were part of a group project, and you started to feel as though other members weren't pulling their weight, how would you handle this situation?"

This can be a frustrating feeling. Maybe there's a group project that includes five people, but there's that one guy who is not pulling his weight. Alternatively, perhaps everyone else is doing all the work and not letting you have the chance to thrive. Your interviewer wants to know how you would handle it if you found yourself in either of these scenarios.

"First, I would address whether there are issues within myself. Am I not delegating tasks properly? Is there a lack of communication? I would ensure I was doing everything I could on my part, and then address issues within the group. I would do it one on one and pull people aside to have personal conversations about the project. If I felt like I wasn't having the opportunity to pull my weight and others were too controlling or were doing the work for me, I would take the same steps."

"What is a strong value that you have that is only related to a working environment?"

When we think of values, we might first think of religion, politics, or philosophy. You won't need to think of this for a question about your working values, however. They want to know what is important to you. How would you describe your work ethic? What is something that you always remind yourself when the going gets tough at work? This is another question specific to you, and there are a few ways you can answer. Here is one of them:

"One value that's important to me is persistence. Sometimes things don't go as planned, and you might have moments of failure, but I always remind myself to try again. If something consistently is not working, then I'll look for a different way to solve the problem. The more I focus on getting back on my feet and continuing the fight, the easier it is to achieve my goals. Even if I fail nine times, the 10th time might be the time I succeed, so it's always important for me to continue on."

"What traits do you think an employee in this specific position should have?"

This is an important question because it will be specific to the employees and what you know about the company already. It shows them what you really think that you will be doing in the position if hired. The question is not just about you, it's about the position. You should put yourself in the perspective of the person conducting the interview, making it easier to see what they might be looking for. When you can do this, it becomes easier to know what a good answer would be. You might base this on a job description that you saw, or it could simply be something that you gathered as you discussed different things throughout the interview. Your response might be something like this:

"I think that it's important for an employee in this position to be reliable. There are several people depending on them, and it seems as though there will be some high-pressure scenarios. If they can't be trusted professionally and personally, then that can put a wedge in the working environment."

"Can you sell me the chair that you are sitting on at the moment?"

This is a question that might be specific to those who are interviewing for a sales position. Even if you won't be working with sales, numbers, or customers at all, it can still be a question that pops up. It is one that will show how well you can try and persuade someone. Are you a good schmoozer? Do you have a creative mindset that helps you to see the benefits even in something as mundane as a chair? They will ask questions like this especially if you are in sales, but the question might differ in how it is presented. They might say something like, "Sell me this pencil", or ask you to sell another object that's around. Your sales pitch might look like this:

"This chair is great for anyone who is looking to sit down. We all could use a break, and when we do decide to get that moment of rest, then this chair is going to be your top choice. It has a cushioned top that makes it comfortable for your bottom, especially for those sitting for long periods of time. It has features where you can adjust the height of the chair, so anyone can benefit from it. Not only does it have great comfort features, but it's aesthetically pleasing as well. Why don't you give it a try for yourself?"

"Is it more important for people to like you in a managerial position, or for people to fear you?"

This is a common question, especially if you are going to be interviewing for a managerial position. It's a frequent discussion of whether or not a manager is supposed to be feared or if they should be liked. Do you want to be the boss that's popular with everyone or is it more important that they become obedient and respect your authority? The best way to answer this is that you should be right in the middle of both.

Chapter 6: Questions on Salary, Promotion and Benefits

How much was your last salary?

Most times, this question is hardly asked during job interviews. However, it is exclusively for people whose curriculum vitae show that they have been working. This is why this question is not asked to job seekers whose application packages show that they are fresh or new in the labor market. If the above question is asked, it is expected that the job you applied for should have higher and better prospects than the past ones. This means that the salary of the prospective job should be higher than your past salaries. If the difference is too wide, you may be considered under qualified for the job. You will be considered overqualified for the job if the salary of your past job is also higher than that of the job you applied for. But the exact difference, most likely, will be unknown to you since you know of the past salary alone. If you had/have a job with a good salary, mention the amount. Do not exaggerate or inflate your past salary because you may not have sufficient evidence, especially bank documents, to defend your false claim, if it is requested. Besides, some employers confirm their applicants' claims on salary prior to making a job offer. However, if your last salary is far below your salary expectation from the prospective job, politely appeal to the interviewer to wave the question aside.

Sample Answers

I am a fresh graduate. So, I have not been on salary as an employee.

I will crave your indulgence to wave this question aside because I am more concerned about the future than the past.

About how much do you expect to be paid as salary?

Try as much as you can to find the salary the organization is will be willing to pay if you are offered an appointment. Your ability to achieve this will help you not to overprice or underprice when you are asked this question. If, however, you were unable to find the salary structure of the organization and the amount the organization will be willing to pay if you are offered the appointment, you should apply caution in answering this question.

The first caution to apply is to avoid mentioning anything about compensation or remuneration, before the question is asked. If salary-related issue should arise, let it be raised by the interviewer. Do not be in a haste in responding to this question. You should not give a specific answer to this question because the amount you mention may be too high or too low. In other words, you may overprice or underprice. You may not be considered for the job if the amount you mention is too high, as the employer may be afraid that you cannot be at home with the organization with the amount it can afford to pay. You may also be rejected on the ground that your standard is below that of the company, if the amount you mention is too low. One of the best approaches to answering this question is to give an open and unspecific answer. Another approach is to tell the interviewer that you have insufficient information to estimate your salary. If, however, you belong to a professional body that has a standard for the remuneration of different categories of its members, you can cite their recommendation/standard. The sample answers below reflect these categories of answers.

Sample Answers

I believe the salaries of your employees are determined by your corporate policy, and accepting your policy is a requisite for being an employee of your organization.

All other things equal, I know that the salary of an employee is determined by a variety of factors. This includes the value/worth of the employee, the status of the organization and the responsibilities and challenges of the job. I do not have enough information to comment on the salary, as I know of the first factor only - my value.

I am a member of the Institute of Chartered Accountants. The institute specifies that members who have my qualifications should be paid a minimum of Nabc,000 per annum. I expect that my salary should be within that range.

Is salary among the factors that determine the satisfaction you derive from a job?
Sample Answer

Though my salary has a role to play in making me happy in a job, it is not the most important thing to me about work. I am more interested in the career prospects of the job and its impact on my personal development.

How often do you expect increase in your salary?

Sample Answer

I believe this would be determined by a number of factors. This includes the policy of the company, my productivity in the organization and the overall success of the company.

How would you justify your salary?

Sample Answer

I expect to be paid from the money I make for the company, and I know that the organization will remain in existence only when the employees generate more money than they are paid. I will justify my income by ensuring that my services to the company surpass my remuneration.

What are your expectations if you are hired?

This question is not as simple as it appears to be. Just as you (should) have some expectations from the job you applied for and your prospective employer, the organization also has its expectations from you. However, you should choose a job because of your expectations from it but justify your interest in the job by emphasising the interest and expectations of the prospective employer. The expectations organizations are delighted with are employees' contributions to their success. Hence, do not say, "I expect the company to be prompt in the payment of salary". Also do not say, "I hope the company will soon increase my salary". You should also avoid saying, "I expect to be promoted very soon". Also avoid saying, "I hope the company will sponsor my vacations". No organization will offer you an appointment because of your expectations from it. Every prospective employer's interest in a job seeker is determined by its expectations - the value the job seeker will add to its organization. This is the area your answer should focus.

Sample Answers

I expect to be an invaluable asset to your organization if I am offered an appointment.

I hope to assist the company to the best of my ability in achieving her organizational goals.

If the interviewer insists on knowing your expectations from the job which will profit you, you should tell him about what you hope to profit from the job if you get the appointment. The expectation should have long term significance. Such question may be, **"Do you have other expectations from this job?"**

Sample Answer

I hope this job will afford me the opportunity to advance my career, if I get the appointment.

How soon do you hope to be promoted?

Sample Answer

I believe that my promotion will be determined by the policy of the company. I also know that my performance also has a role to play in earning my promotion because I will not be qualified for promotion until I am overqualified for the position I occupy.

Has your salary been delayed before?

Sample Answer

My past employers were very prompt in payment.

Has your salary ever been reduced?

Sample Answer

I am yet to have that experience in a place of work.

What would you do if your salary is delayed for any reason?

Sample Answer

It depends on the factor that is responsible for the delay. As an accountant, I will always know when the company is making profit and when it is having financial challenges. I am confident that the organization cannot afford to risk her reputation by owing the employees at a time it is making profit, and I also know that this organization has a reputation for accelerated growth.

Will you leave us if you get a better offer?

"**How soon would you join us if you are employed?**" Both questions are related, likewise their answers. Your answers to both questions should cohere. In the book, it was advised that you should be very careful with your answer because the prospective employer will not expect you to (promise to) start the new job immediately if you claimed to be working with an organization. It was also remarked that it is wrong to resign from a job without prior notification in order to join a new organization. In addition, it was noted that the interviewer may be afraid that you are not saying the truth or that you will frustrate their organizational activities with an abrupt resignation if you get a better job while with them, if you promise to start immediately. While answering the question, **"Will you leave us if you get a better offer?"**, do not be in a haste with denying that you will not accept a better offer if it comes your way in the future. Remember, you aspire for progress, and one of the ways of achieving that is getting a job that is better than the one you applied for, even if you are offered appointment. You should be mindful of the fact that the interviewer is not ignorant of this. Consequently, exercise diplomacy and caution in answering this question.

Sample Answer

I desire progress in life. I also desire to advance my career. I know that I may not achieve that without getting a better job. However, I do not consider a job as a better one just because it has a higher remuneration. There are other conditions like job security and future prospects which are more important to me. However, I will not be in a haste to leave your organization so that I will not frustrate your activities. Since I will likely not spend the rest of my working years in your organization, I will respect your policy whenever I am about to resign.

Chapter 7: Managing Third-Party Recruiters

If you have not applied for jobs in a while, or if you are relatively new to the job market, then you need to pay close attention to this chapter.

Who Are Third-Party Recruiters?

Third-party recruiters (also known as headhunters, external recruiters, staffing or talent acquisition specialists, talent agents, among other titles) are professionals who companies hire to help them find candidates for open positions. The recruiters can either work for small or larger organizations or they can be independent contractors.

Regardless of where they work, it is important to understand that third-party recruiters work for the **companies they are helping**, not you. They have a financial interest in placing you, therefore, all of their advice to you must be taken with this in mind.

Well, one of the work-arounds for companies (other than ATS) is to have these external recruiters take care of this part of the process for them, so they don't have to comb through piles of résumés. Recruiters will do the initial screening of candidates and then present companies with several options, so the process is more manageable and efficient.

There are both positives and negatives with having third-party recruiters as part of your job search. Let's discuss both.

The Positives

1. If you connect with a recruiter and he or she winds up sending your résumé to a company, then you are substantially increasing your chances of your résumé being seen and then getting called for an interview.

2. A lot of times these recruiters have established relationships with the companies they represent which also means they have a good idea of what a particular hiring manager is looking for and what types of questions you can expect during the interview. This is incredibly valuable information.

3. Recruiters will help negotiate your salary and other benefits on your behalf so you do not need to

speak with the company directly about any of those topics.

4. If you do not get an interview or an offer, and you enjoyed working with the recruiter, then you now have a new contact for possible future opportunities.

The Negatives

1. Recruiters only get paid (or earn a decent portion of their compensation) when you agree to a company's offer. In other words, they work on commission. Therefore, they may try to justify a weak dollar offer or a company's unwillingness to give you an extra week of vacation in the hopes that you'll sign your offer letter so they can get paid. Only you know what's really best for you.

2. Low barrier to entry. In today's world, almost anyone can be a recruiter and the market is, therefore, saturated with them. It can be a very cut-throat business when there are so many players which is why it's important to understand the potential pitfalls.

3. Some recruiters will use under-handed tactics to try and extract information from you that they can potentially use for their own purposes. More on this in a minute.

Over the years, I have heard (and personally experienced) many stories about questionable, rude, and/or unethical behavior toward job seekers by external recruiters. Recruiters who behave in this way are not worth your time. Only spend time working with the true professionals.

How to Connect with Recruiters

You can connect with recruiters in two ways: they reach out to you (usually via LinkedIn or your email) or you actively seek them out. Let's take each scenario separately.

They Reach out to You

This is common especially when your LinkedIn profile is updated. They are looking for potential candidates who may be willing to entertain the idea of switching companies.

If you are contacted by a recruiter, first make sure they want to discuss a **specific** position and you get the job description from them in writing before sending your résumé along. The reason this is important is because there are some recruiters out there who will "fish" for professionals to add into their databases and will lie about having an open position just to get your résumé and other details.

Story: Here is an actual email exchange to illustrate what I mean:

A recruiter sent an email with a brief, generic job description for a position in a job seeker's general geographic location. The company and location were not revealed.

Job Seeker: Thank you for the email. Can you tell me who the company is and the location?
No response from the recruiter. Job Seeker follows up with another email three days later.

Recruiter: This is a semi-confidential search in that we are disclosing the company once we have had a pre-qualification discussion via phone.

Job Seeker: I understand. I'd like to learn more. When is a good time to chat?

Recruiter: Are you actively looking?

Job Seeker: I'm keeping my options open. I'm free Thursday morning. Will that work?
No response from the recruiter.

No decent recruiter is going to drag his feet when there is an interested candidate for an open position. This exchange was highly suspect from the radio silence the recruiter gave the job seeker after the recruiter initially reached out. Fortunately for the job seeker, no real time was wasted and the recruiter only got the fact that the job seeker was interested. It doesn't matter because that recruiter has already proven not to be worth the job seeker's time.

Look out for nonsense like this.

There are right ways to build relationships and there are many wrong ways to go about it. Just be diligent and aware like you would when someone you don't know reaches out and starts asking for sensitive information.

You Reach out to Them

If you find you are having trouble searching on your own, either because of time or other constraints, then you can proactively reach out to recruiters as they may be able to help you.

There are also independent recruiters who are easily found on LinkedIn.

If they're smart, they will take your call and if they're professional, they'll be honest with you regarding whether they can ultimately help you then or in the future. In these cases, you will send them your résumé so they can get a clear understanding of your background and what you're looking to do next.

Note: In either case, never hand over your résumé unless you first have their agreement, in writing, that they will not send your résumé to any company without your written permission. Any good recruiter will understand this.

<u>What's the big deal if they send out my résumé? It can't hurt, right?</u>

Wrong.

The reason this clarification is necessary is because there are some recruiters who will send your résumé to companies without you even knowing! The problem with this is the company receiving your résumé does not know that you did not give consent, and then you can potentially look bad (without you even knowing), especially if a recruiter is over the line or aggressive with the company.

Don't let someone else tarnish your reputation with unprofessionalism. Guard your résumé closely and only give it out directly to companies or recruiters whom you trust and/or are comfortable with.

Speaking with Recruiters

Once recruiters have your résumé, you will most likely have a call with them so they can learn a little more about you and what you're looking to do next. This is very common and should be an easy conversation. The initial phone call should be casual but professional and fairly brief. You should not be surprised by any questions or made to feel uncomfortable in any way.

Be cognizant of how the conversation is going. A good recruiter will want to know your work history, where you are looking to go next in your career, how far you would be willing to commute, and possibly what your salary requirements would be.

Questions to Watch out for

Unfortunately, this is not always the case. All of the below questions (among others), including the many variations, are red flags. All of these questions are meant to work against you as negotiating leverage for a company; or are just plain nosy and rude.

Do not answer any of these and, if more than one comes up during a conversation, don't continue to engage with this particular recruiter. They are not worth your time.

Note: The same goes for company employees. They should <u>not</u> be asking you these types of questions either.

• What is your current salary?

• What is your salary history?

• What is the lowest salary that you'll accept?

• Do you have a family/kids?

• Do you own a home?

• How old are you?

• What year did you graduate college?

• Where are you from originally?

While some of these questions may come across as a recruiter innocently wanting to get to know you better, the fact is that <u>all</u> of these questions are offensive and none of his business.

If you reached out to a recruiter, then you will discuss what you are looking to do next as well as whether there are any current openings that might be a potential fit. And, if you are speaking to him about a specific role, then you will talk about your work history, your salary requirements, and also work to learn as much about the new role as he can tell you. That's it.

All of those other questions are totally irrelevant and, in some cases, illegal.

Recruiters are not your career counselor, friend, or mentor. They are **agents for a company** and are trying to earn a commission by placing you. Your relationship with a recruiter is also a *business relationship*. You don't need to answer offensive questions to be seriously considered for open positions, so don't allow them to make you feel small in any way. You are in total control of these interactions.

Finally, like with many of the topics in this book, use your gut. If recruiters (or anyone else you connect with) are making any types of disparaging or negative comments about you or your work history, you don't have to tolerate it. Your work history is what it is and you have nothing to apologize for. Don't get involved with someone who doesn't take the time to understand who you are and what you are looking to do next. Do not get drawn into a bad relationship. If it doesn't feel right, walk away and cut off all communication. There are plenty of good recruiters out there with whom you can work.

Knowledge Is Power

This book, especially this chapter, is meant to empower you on your journey to your next job. The more information you have about all of these moving parts, the more powerful you will be which will quickly translate into confidence.

Confidence impacts everything we do and everyone we meet in a positive way. Having confidence in yourself is the keystone to becoming a strong and successful job seeker, and this confidence will serve you best during the most important part of the process, the interview.

Chapter 8: The Negotiation_

When this time of talking about salary and wages comes up, you will likely encounter some negotiation. Negotiation is something that many people are afraid of. People are afraid that if they ask for too much, they will offend the employer. People are also afraid that if they do not ask for enough, they will get offered lower than they would have if they would have just waited for the employer to offer first. Negotiating is still extremely important. Negotiation is the way that you can get what you want and the way that you can get what you deserve. It is the way to get the best possible salary and wage the company can offer you. Negotiation is a way to stand up for yourself and to show what you are truly worth it. In this chapter, we are going to look into negotiation and how to do it successfully.

Negotiating successfully

First, let's look into what you need to know about negotiation. Negotiation is not about arguing over wages; it's about knowing your worth. One of the things that you need to do to negotiate well is to know what you are worth before going into an interview. Decide what you would want to make, and stick to it. You know that you are a great worker and that you are worth more than what some jobs are offering. You need to know the salary that you are comfortable with and the salary that you are looking for. If you do not, you will likely get a wage that you are not happy with. This may possibly be the cause of you not having the ability to be happy in your dream job. It can be the cause of stress in your life.

You may not always get what you negotiate for, but at least you know you tried. If you negotiate, you know that you are getting the best the company can offer you. If you do not negotiate, you may not be getting the best. This is because companies will usually offer you a lower amount of money that they are planning to pay first. The company will offer you a lower amount to see if you take it. This is not meant to be offensive toward you or to any other employees; it is just simply meant to save the company some money. The company likely knows they are starting out with the lowest possible wage, and they probably know the highest amount they can go to as well. For this, they usually expect there to be some type of negotiation involved in the hiring process.

Since companies are expecting a negotiation, it is not something that you need to be afraid of. When you negotiate, it actually shows companies you are confident and that you know your worth. Even though it causes companies to pay you more money and lowers their profit, many companies may actually be happy about the fact that you want to negotiate. It shows you can stand up for yourself, that you are serious about the position, and that you care about how you feel in the position as well. If you do not negotiate, the company may feel as though you are not as serious about the position as other applicants. For this, you might as well always at least try to negotiate salary during a job offer.

Another thing to think about when negotiating during a job offer is that you do not lose anything if they say no. It is not like they're going to lower their wage that they previously offered you. If you asked to make more money and you'll get it, great. Then your negotiations were worth it. If you ask for more money and you do not get it, okay. More than likely, the company will not be upset with you at all, and you will still be at the same wage you were before you asked. For this, it is easy to see that negotiation does not hurt you in any way. It can be uncomfortable at first, but maybe either leads to a better result or the same result, never worse.

When you are going to a job interview, you should know that negotiations could happen either during that interview or afterward during the job offer. You should never bring up wages during a job interview. If wages are brought up, they will be brought up by the person who is conducting the interview. If the person conducting the interview brings up wages, you can feel free to negotiate. This is because if the person who is conducting the interview starts talking about wages, it is likely that they are interested in hiring you. If you talk to them about negotiation during this time, it can save you from coming back for another trip if the salary is too low for what you need. If you ignore the chance to negotiate, you may not have a chance to negotiate later on.

Sometimes, wages are not brought up in interviews at all. If wages are not brought up in your interview, do not mention them on your own. If you get a job offer, they will be offered then. It is possible that the job is not interested in hiring you and why they're not talking about wages, or it could be that their policy is to wait to discuss wages until the job offer happens. Either way, you should wait until the company brings the wage issue up first.

If the wage is brought up during your job offer, then this is a completely appropriate time to negotiate. If you get a job offer, they will likely tell you how much you will make. You can decide if you want to take the job or leave it with this number. If you do not like the number they give you, you can negotiate it and see if they can give you more. Either you will end up making more money, or you will end up making the same amount you were going to make before you asked for the possibility of the salary to change. You will never make less money just from asking a question. For this, if we just brought up during a job offer, you might as well try to negotiate it.

As an example, you could say, " I am focusing on jobs in the variety of $70,000 per year". If you say this, the job will know exactly how much you were looking to make each year.

Again, it is important to have this number picked out before you go to the interview or before you get the call for the job offer. This is because you want to have the number ready in your mind before you have to say it. You want to think this number over to make sure that you are getting as much as possible while still being reasonable. For this, you probably want to choose the number when you have some time to think about it and not during an interview or job offer.

When you get this number in your head, stick to it. Do not lower it just because you want to take a position. Do not lower it just because you do not feel like negotiating. You know what you are worth and you need to stick to that. You should make what you feel you deserve. If you do not, you could resent your job later on with it.

When you are negotiating, remember to be confident. For this, if you are their top choice for the job opening, you will likely get more money than what they are offering. They could always go with someone who did not want to make as much money, but then they would be sacrificing the quality of the candidates that they were hiring. Most companies will not do this, so you do not need to worry about it.

When you tell the employer how much you want to make, they may offer you a lower amount. If they do this, consider negotiating. Try to meet in the middle. If the company can only offer you so much, there are other ways that you can get up to the salary that you want. To give an example, if you ask for $70,000 per year, but they can only offer you $65,000 per year due to their budget size, you could ask them for a $5,000 sign on bonus to reach your annual wage. You could tell them that this will get you up to the wage that you need for this year, and you will talk about next year when that time comes.

Another way that you can negotiate is their benefits. If a job can't pay you how much you want, consider asking them for extra vacation time. Most people are willing to work for less money if it means they can have more time off of work. As an example, if you took a $5,000 per year pay cut, you could get an extra week or two of vacation time to make up for it. This would give you more time to do things that you love to do, like to stay home with your family or travel. This extra time may possibly be worth the pay cut. If it is, consider negotiating with benefits if the job can't give you the wage that you were looking for. This may help you to feel better about making less money because you know you are still getting something out of it. It will also help you to know that the company is doing everything they can to give you what you need, even if they can't pay you the wage that you want to make.

When you are negotiating, things may not always go well. There may be times when you have to tell a job no when they offer you a number you cannot afford to take. If a job offers you a lower amount than you are willing to accept, and they're not in a position to negotiate with you, do not feel bad about turning them down. This not only means you need to fight for what you are worth, but it also means you need to walk away sometimes when a company is unwilling to give it to you. If you cannot negotiate a deal that you are happy with, consider moving on. If the company does not see what you are worth, they simply do not deserve you. This can be hard at first because you can see a company that seems like it would be your dream workplace, and then you find out that they cannot pay you as much as you want to make. However, another company will always come up sooner or later that sees your worth. A company will come up that actually deserves you. You just need to be patient and wait for it to happen.

When you are negotiating, remember to have a number in place before you go into the conversation. Otherwise, save this number for the job offer. You can discuss it and negotiate about it at that time. Also, remember it is okay to negotiate. They will not get mad at you for doing so, and you will not lose anything. You will either come out making more money or the same amount of money that you were before you talked about it. You will never make less money after negotiations. Remember when negotiating, you can likely meet in the middle. If the company cannot give you the amount you need, consider asking for a bonus or for additional benefits to make up for it. Also, remember that if your negotiations do not work, feel free to move on. You will find a company that knows your worth and that treats you the way you deserve.

Negotiation can feel scary, but it doesn't have to be.

Chapter 9: How to Handle Closing Questions

"If you were hired, what would you seek to accomplish in the first three months in the new job?"

Employers ask this question to gauge how you think about ramping up on your new role, how fast you are going to complete the onboarding process, and the types of standards and goals you have set for yourself, especially it being a new environment.

Remember that this time is also when you will be learning a lot about your responsibilities, your leaders, as well as the workplace etiquette. You will be adjusting and learning how to fit into the larger organization.

A part of your own interview preparation should be understanding what the particular job responsibilities and company structure will be like and to align it with your goals in order to ace this question.

Clearly, the longer it would take you to contribute significantly to the organization, the less admirable you would be. Therefore, avoid being vague or showing how you will probably still be adapting to the new environment. Employers today are interested in the fast-paced, innovative, and easily adaptable personnel.

A good answer would be, for instance, "Besides getting to know the team and fully tuning to the role, there is a lot more I'd like to accomplish in the first three months. In the first month, I want to learn the design of our marketing projects. After two months, I want to redesign and launch a project by tuning the efforts of the team, and after three months, I want to be able to track the growth of our marketing efforts."

"What questions haven't I asked you?"

Employers make this inquiry to assess your interest in the field and your enthusiasm and commitment to improving yourself as a worker in the industry. It offers a chance to showcase your ability to decipher information and establish anything you feel is important that they have not touched. Pointing out such a thing is what sets you apart and shows that you know what brought you here, how different you are, and your planned contributions.

Naturally, a person to be considered will be the one who seems truly invested in the industry and their personal development.

Be sure to emphasize your stage of career development, how you want to develop yourself professionally, and your long-term goals.

Avoid arrogance like showing you are the pinnacle of development with nothing extra to learn. Do not emphasize your idealized salary and fun job.

You could say, for instance, "My main focus is to continue developing my leadership and organizational skills, and I believe in constantly challenging myself to achieve more. My vision is around the big picture, and I want to exploit that ability the best possible way."

"What questions do you have for me?"

As the interview comes to a close, the interviewer is most likely to ask if you have any questions for them. It may feel as if you have covered everything in the course of your interview, but it is paramount to respond to this question rather than decline.

Your response should be guided by the knowledge of with whom you are interviewing. If it is your potential manager, then you can ask questions about the responsibilities of the position. If it is human resource personnel, however, you can ask questions generally about the organization.

You should prepare a list of various questions to ask during this phase in case some of them are addressed during the interview. Your response to this question will tell how keen you were during the conversation.

About the company you can ask:

- Can you talk a bit about the company culture?

- What are the goals of the company for the upcoming year?

About the role you can ask:

- Could you please share more about the daily routine responsibilities of the job?

- What is the major indicator of accomplishment in this job, from your perspective?

Avoid questions on topics such as off-work activities, interviewer's personal life, minor things you could answer yourself, as well as salary and benefits.

"Why should we hire you?"

By posing this question, employers are really asking to hear what you have to offer them and what other candidates may not. You should take this opportunity to reinstate your skills and prowess in doing some of the tasks you believe you can do best. Remember that the reason they need to hire someone is for them to solve a particular problem. Hence, your goal should be to show that you are the best person to solve their problem.

To prepare for this question, match your qualifications with the job requirements. Then, use anecdotes to illustrate your qualifications. Anyone can say that they have strong communication skills, but few can tell a story about how they have used those skills to negotiate a deal and successfully complete a major project.

Be sure to focus on your uniqueness to make yourself stand out among other applicants. Also, identify skills that may add extra value, including volunteer experiences that could have provided you with a unique outlook.

However, avoid bragging and assuming that you are the summit of progress. Present your response politely.

A typical answer would be:

"I feel that my experience in this industry and my ability to utilize a unique and work-related capability makes me a good match for this role."

Then explain how in a recent role you used this ability.

"When can you start working?"

This question also comes in the form of, "How much notice do you need to give to your current employer?" which especially applies to candidates who are currently working in another company.

This question can feel exciting and promising, but do not take it as the guarantee of a job offer. This question is not necessarily an indication that you will be offered this job.

The first thing to avoid is sounding desperate or like you are too eager, since this behavior may make employers suspicious of your motives for the job.

Even if they have selected you already but they do not tell you when they need you to start, some flexibility is allowed in determining a date that is good for you. If they give a date, inform them whether you are okay with it and avoid making a commitment you cannot keep.

If you are currently employed, the answer depends on the amount of notice that you need to give your current boss, or any other plans you may have. An appropriate answer would be, "My employer requires me to give one-month notice before I leave, so I would be able to start on [insert date]."

If you are not employed, you may want to begin working immediately to settle your bills. But do not underestimate the time you might need to gracefully tune yourself into the work mood. An appropriate answer would be, "I would greatly appreciate a few days, say a week or two, to clear the decks before I begin, but I can be flexible if you need me a little earlier."

"Would you work holidays and weekends?"

Simple as it looks, this question can effectively set aside individuals to be hired and those to be rejected. Some industries require workers to be flexible and be able to juggle work and other commitments because of frequent projects or long hours of operation needed at times.

Some tips when answering this question include being realistic about your time, but give your response a positive spin. For instance, you can say, "I have no problem working on weekends or holidays as long as I can schedule myself as early as possible."

Also, know your limits. Employers need confidence in a candidate who can keep time commitments. For instance, you can say, "Due to family commitments, I cannot commit to working every weekend and every holiday, but I can certainly give some of the days if need be."

You do not want to say a flat no and give your interviewer the impression that you cannot give up some of your free time for work purposes. Industries such as hospitality require this element.

Ideally, show some flexibility in your schedule, indicate that you have time management skills, and be confident and tactful. Avoid committing to a schedule that you cannot keep, and do not disclose more information about your schedule than necessary.

"How would you fire someone?"

This counter-intuitive question is raised especially when you are looking for a management position. The recruiter wants to assess if you have really got what it takes. Are you able to deliberate and fire an employee when necessary or just ignore the problem? Also, they are concerned that you will fire someone in a way that upholds the rights of the company and confidentiality of the employee when firing them.

Take this opportunity to demonstrate your management style and re-emphasize the leadership skills (such as emotional intelligence) you expressed in earlier parts of the interview. Show that you would never take firing someone lightly.

Avoid being mean when role-playing, as it is not the time to channel your perceived inner strength.

Rather, respectfully show that you are firm and ready to make reasons for firing clear.

A reasonable way to fire is to say something like, "I'd first of all try to see if there is anything I can do to prevent having to fire the individual, such as constant communication and performance review. If it comes to the point that I have to terminate their contract, I'd engage with them privately without the knowledge of any other employee and explain the reason for termination."

Chapter 10: Bonus Questions

You really can never be too prepared in an interview. While you don't want to over-practice and make yourself nervous, it's still a good idea to keep up with potential questions and focus on thinking of all the loose ends that need to be tied up before the interview.

It's encouraged to come up with your own ideas of questions that the person conducting the interview would potentially ask. When you can put yourself in their shoes, you will be able to easily see the kinds of things that they might believe are the most important.

"How do you manage your stress levels?"

Stress is something that everyone feels. Even when we try our best to manage it, stress can still creep into our lives in seemingly small ways. The answer to this question is not about trying to deny that you get stressed. Instead, give a realistic method that you use in order to alleviate some of the symptoms. Here is a good answer:

"I make sure that I am managing my time first and foremost. When I can prepare and prevent it helps to keep the stress from creeping up in the first place. I do know my limits, however, so when I am feeling stressed I will do my best to take a break so I can come back with a clear mind, better ready to focus."

"How do you prioritize your tasks?"

We talked a lot about prioritization, and how you will need to do it first when you are organizing anything. But how exactly might you prioritize tasks? This helps the person conducting the interview to determine what's important to you and how you will gauge whether or not something needs your attention. Here's an example of what you might consider saying:

"I prioritize tasks first by how important they are. Then, I will number them and try to base what I'll do around this list. I also look to see if there are any tasks that I can quickly do to get out of the way. Sometimes it makes it easier to focus on the most important things if some of the smaller fluff is out of the way. I always ensure that I am focused on managing my time above all else."

"What steps do you take if someone you don't like in the office is really bothering you?"

We have all had that one coworker who seems to get really annoying. Maybe they chew their gum loudly every day, or perhaps they like to glance at your computer screen over your shoulder. Whatever it might be, you don't have to mention what they do that's annoying! What they will be looking for is how you might be able to handle this situation. Here's something you could say:

"I would first make sure that I am showing patience to them. It is easier to be annoyed with things on bad days, maybe if I were stressed about something outside of work. I would do my best to be patient and not let the little things bother or distract me. If I had a close relationship with them and felt comfortable, I might say something, like 'Would you mind not chewing your gum so loudly?' If not, then I would avoid the situation, and maybe wear headphones if permitted."

"What did you do to prepare for this interview?"

This is a good question that kind of breaks the awkward wall that was created surrounding this interaction. We don't always talk about how this can be a stressful time that we have to do our best to prepare for! This is a time when you will want to be honest above all else. Here's a good thing to say:

"I started my morning making sure I got enough rest before heading here so I could be relaxed. I got ready, got dressed in what I picked out this morning, and had a nice breakfast. The night before I made sure to go over my resume once more and freshen up on what questions I might be asked. On the way here, I listened to some relaxing music to reduce stress so that I would be able to relax and give honest answers throughout!"

"What are you hardest on yourself about?"

This is a good question to ask because it allows the person conducting the interview to get an idea of the kind of things you might personally struggle with. They will want to ensure that whatever you are saying is not something that will affect your job, but they also want to hear some personal honesty from you. Here's something that you might consider telling them:

"I feel as though I never do enough. Even when I have a fully productive day, I feel like there was more I could do. I think this is just because I understand how precious time can be and I want to make the most of my life, but that sometimes can cause me to be stressed and feel like I always need to be doing more!"

"What TV or movie character do you most relate to?"

This is a great question. It lets people understand first what it is that you enjoy. Which movies or shows do you like? What books do you read? After that, it can help them relate your personality to someone that they might know. When you answer this question, you will be able to give them a familiar idea of the type of personality that you might have. Here's an example, but make sure to pick something specific to you as well:

"I would have to say that I am like Ariel from The Little Mermaid. I am curious about learning more about the world, I enjoy swimming, and I have a diverse group of friends!"

"What is the last object that you fixed?"

This is a good question because it shows that you are a problem-solver. Even if you will never have to fix anything in the position that you are applying for, it still lets them know that you do have some handy skills and that you know how to get yourself out of certain situations. Answer this honestly, but here's an example of something you might wish to say:

"The last thing that I fixed was my garbage disposal. For about a week it wasn't working, and I was too afraid to stick my hand down in there in case that would be the moment it started working! Finally, I turned off the power and got a heavy-duty glove to help resolve the issue! My hand came out safe and the disposal is working better than ever!"

"When is the last time you lost something? Did you find it?"

This is a question to show your level of responsibility. It's easy to say that we hold onto all sorts of responsibility, but at the same time, practical questions like this actually help to show what your level of accountability is. Try and think of what the last thing you actually lost was and find a way to relate it to this job. Here's an answer that you might choose to say:

"The last thing that I lost were my house keys. I went to grab them and realized that they weren't in their usual spot. Then I retraced my steps and realized I had left them in the pocket of my pants which was in the dryer! They weren't lost for more than a few minutes, but I was able to remember everything I did so I could easily find them."

"Can you describe to me how you would make a PB and J sandwich?"

This question is not because the person conducting the interview is legitimately curious about how to make a PB and J sandwich. They might slip an easy question like this in there just to see what you thought process is. Where do you start? Are you going to begin by telling them to spread the peanut butter on the bread and then the jelly? Always start at the very beginning of the process and make sure you thoroughly explain all the steps so that they can really see what your thought pattern is. Here's a great way to answer this:

"First, I would start by gathering my ingredients, and making sure they're there in the first place. I'd place out a plate with two slices of bread, a knife for the peanut butter and then a spoon for the jelly. I'd consider who would be eating this as well. If it were me, I'd go heavy on the PB and light on the jelly. If it were for someone like my little sister, on the other hand, I'd cut the crusts off and make sure to put a scoop of extra jelly. I'd spread the ingredients on the bread and put the two pieces together. I'd serve the sandwich and then clean my utensils, putting my supplies away."

Chapter 11: Follow-Up

After your interview, send a thank you note to the interviewer. My recommendation here is that you send an actual thank you card (something plain) that you purchase at a local store. Ensure that your name and contact information is clearly printed on the inside of the card. If you have more than a few sentences to say, then it would be appropriate to send a personal letter instead of a card (or included with the card). For your thank you card to have any impact on your interview results, you need to send it immediately. If you wait a few days, the employer may have already made a decision before he/she receives your thank you card.

Your thank you card should be just that. Begin by noting how much you enjoyed meeting the interviewer and then thank him/her for considering you for the job.

If you decide to send a letter instead of a card, then you could add statements such as "I left with a better understanding of the role of … at your company." You might also say things like "I believe this position would be a good match for me (and you might state one or two of your best strengths that match the company's needs).

End your letter with a simple statement along the lines of "I look forward to hearing from you further."

If you have a letter of reference that you have not yet shared with the employer, you could insert it into your thank you letter.

It is also appropriate to send your thank you by email, although I would allow a few hours or even half a day to pass before you do this. Keep in mind though that emails tend to get deleted (almost immediately) whereas an actual hard copy thank you note tends to stay on the person's desk (often for a few days).

A question I am constantly asked by job seekers is "Should I call the employer if I haven't heard back within a few days?"

In response to this question, at the end of your interview you should have asked about the next step (and timelines) in the interview process. This information is one of your clues to deciding when to contact an employer after your interview. I would recommend you wait a few days after the deadline that the employer gave to you before calling. Some career experts would even say to wait a week, but I wouldn't go beyond this.

When you call the employer, you could begin the conversation by stating that you believed a decision related to the job was going to be made by such and such date. As this date has now passed, you were wondering if the timeline has been extended or whether a decision has been made.

If you are told that a decision has been made and you were not successful, be genuine in your thanks to the employer for considering you and taking the time to interview you. It would also be beneficial for you to end the conversation by stating your continued interest in working at the company if some other related job should become available.

There is one final note I should mention about what you should be doing after a job interview. Once the interview is over and you have sent your thank you card, then it is important to resume your job search.

I have seen people sit around and do nothing for weeks after a job interview, only to find out they didn't get the job. Not only have they lost the job they were interviewed for, but they have potentially lost some other possible jobs that might have been available while they stopped their job search. Until you have received a definite job offer, persist in your job search.

The reality is that in some job interviews, you will be asked what you expect your salary to be. It is therefore important to research the salary range that could be expected for the position that you are applying for, along with a solid understanding of your own financial needs.

The following page provides some tips on salary negotiations.

SALARY NEGOTIATION TIPS

1. Don't bring up the topic of salary during your first interview unless it is mentioned by the interviewer.

2. Before a job interview, know how much money you need to make (what is your bottom line in order to meet your living expenses?).

3. Research the salary range for the job you are applying for. If you are asked what salary you are expecting, give an amount that falls within this range, or you could even state the range and say that you would be willing to start at a salary that fell within this range. It could be to your benefit to appear to have some flexibility.

4. If you plan on stating a starting salary that is near the top of the range that you researched, then be prepared to explain why you are worth this salary.

5. When salary is being discussed, it is important for you to be aware of any benefits such as health insurance, pension, etc. It would also be useful to gain an understanding of opportunities to increase your base salary such as commissions, incentives, bonuses, or overtime.

6. It is important for you to clearly understand exactly what is expected of you in our job position before you settle on a salary amount.

7. Emphasize your value by talking about how you can help a company to be more profitable.

8. Avoid talking about your needs. It doesn't help to tell the employer about your car payments, or mortgage, student loans, or any other form of personal financial information.

9. Be open to options. Perhaps, there are some creative incentives for meeting specific objectives or goals that could increase your base salary.

Be realistic. If your training and previous job experience doesn't warrant that you should be placed in the top salary range, don't demand it. Whenever you are uncertain about a salary offer, ask for a day or two to think things over.

Chapter 12: Common Mistakes Made During An Interview

Having inappropriate or questionable content in social networking sites.

Remember, organizations do a background check before recruiting any one. About 70% managers in the recruiting department of different organizations have said that candidates make a grave mistake of uploading and posting compromising content in different social networking sites. Through the content, managers get to learn about writing skills and other insights of candidates.

Asking few questions.

This portrays that the concerning person is not interested in the job. The key is to ask not vital but smart questions. This way, you will not come across as a clueless or disinterested person.

Being overconfidence

This is mostly made by the younger generation. It is because they are conditioned and trained to have a strong sense of self-esteem, which most of the time, develops as overconfidence. They often make the interview process, only about them.

Turning Up Late

This should not happen in the first place which is why you don't need to take the chance. Set off very early. Its irritating how, only on the day of your interview that traffic and everything else seems to work against you. If it happens, you had better have such a reasonable excuse that it cannot be ignored. And at every opportunity, call in and let the interviewer know.

Fidgeting with Unnecessary Props

Please! Please! Please! Find a very diplomatic way of hiding your nerves and fears. Don't fidget with the pen, the books, folders, mobile phone, nails, your thigh or beard - don't do it. It sends too many wrong messages. For example, that you may be lying about something, or that you are not confident you can settle in the role, *etc.*

Unclear Answering and Rambling

If you don't know the answer to a question, say so and with a "sorry," but don't rant something totally off track. It isn't really the time to fool your way out.

It can make the interviewer feel his/her intelligence is being insulted. And don't mumble. If the interviewer(s) has to ask what you just said more than three times, then you will start to lose it all on their score-sheet.

Speaking Negatively About Your Current Employer

If you don't have anything good to say about your former employer(s), please don't say anything. It won't go well for you if you do. The potential employer is likely to see himself in the same position when you finally leave their employment.

Discussing Money or Time Off

Unless it is put on the table by the interviewer, avoid as far as possible talking about salary packages, sick and holiday leave, or welfare policies. It soon becomes obvious you are not attending the interview for anything other than for money and people with that kind of dispensation hardly add any value to any role – they simply take!

Not Following Up

This is something not many candidates do after an interview – so the few that do it get an extra advantage. Even if you think your performance at the interview wasn't that great, you should still send the potential employer a short email message to say thank you for the opportunity and that you are still very enthusiastic about getting the job. Don't leave it days after the interview – do it the same day of the interview. The little extra effort only goes to show that you are a cut more serious about the role than all the others.

Assuming an Interview is an Interrogation

Too many interviewees assume that an interview is a process of the interviewer asking a series of questions and the interviewee finding responses to those questions. This is simply not the case. An interview is a two-way process. The employer is as much on trial in an interview as the interviewee. Be prepared to probe the interviewer for information and keep on with follow up questions until you are satisfied with your answers. Remember - this is your career that we're talking about! You don't want to wind up at a company who files for bankruptcy six months after you join, the signs of their impending doom having been painfully obvious to see had you just been a bit more assertive in your line of questioning.

Responding to a question without thinking

Sometimes in an interview we can lose focus. When this happens we either lose track of what we are saying or don't know how to respond to a question. The worst thing to do in this instance is to panic and blurt out the first thing that comes to mind. If you find yourself in this situation, choose a more constructive approach. Win yourself some time by repeating the question out loud to help you to refocus or ask the interviewer to repeat it. If you've forgotten what you are saying, admit as much to the interviewer and ask him/her to repeat the question. Never try to muddle through without having a focus on a question as it will only confuse you and the interviewer.

Not doing your pre-interview homework

Failing to make time to do your research on the employer, or planning how you can emphasize the qualities on your resume, or what questions you should ask the employer when prompted then you'll be doing yourself a huge injustice. The better prepared you are to answer questions about yourself, your career and your personality then the more likely you are to impress the interviewer and land that job.

Being Arrogant

Knowing within yourself that you have answers to all the questions being asked and being happy with it should not make you come across as arrogant. Don't start speaking or behaving like you've already got the job – you might be unpleasantly surprised. It will be far more profitable to your chances if you keep calm throughout the interview. If you know something that a panelist or interviewer doesn't know, control yourself. Don't let it show on the large screen of your ego. Nothing puts off a potential employer than an arrogant candidate – from the point it is first exhibited, most interviewers simply shut down from listening to you any further.

Turning the Weakness Question into A Positive

When interviewers ask about your weaknesses, they know we all have a few, so it's quite insulting of their intelligence if you try to paint yourself as someone without any. Instead, I suggest to think about a weakness that can be improved, but which does not impact on any of the core requirements of the job you are applying for.

Get caught lying.

A definite guarantee that you will not get the job is to lie during the job interview. If you are going to make a bold claim or state something that is not true, seriously think about your chances of getting away with it. Companies run background checks on potential hires. Whether it is about your credentials, accomplishments or your work history, honesty will usually be the best policy. It's tempting I know, but honestly what would it prove? If you lie about qualifications the employer will find out. If you lie about your career history the employer will find out. If you lie about your knowledge and experience you could end up getting into a very embarrassing situation in the interview itself!

Inappropriate humor.

Be confident, but avoid cracking jokes unnecessarily or saying things probably best left unsaid. A little touch of humor could work in your favor, provided that it is appropriate to the context of the interview. You do not need to be funny, especially when it is at the expense of appropriateness and formality. The last thing you want is for the hiring manager to think you are not serious about the job opportunity.

Getting personal.

A job interview is a formal meeting to assess if you are the right fit for a job. Everything in your personal life, your subjective opinions and how you are feeling should be left outside the door, and not be brought up during the interview.

Not appearing attentive.

It goes without saying that you should give 101% of your attention to the interviewer and respond to questions accordingly. Not smiling, playing with something on the table, bad posture, no eye contact, and fidgeting too much are behaviors indicating you are not paying attention. Additionally, checking your phone or answering calls are almost definitely job interview deal breakers.

Ask when the interview will end.

Nothing says "I don't care about this job and I am just wasting your time" like asking the interviewer how long the interview will be, or when will it end. You will also be doing just as much damage by constantly looking at your watch. When you are called in for a job interview, you are expected to make time for it, if you really want to get the job.

Bad-mouthing previous companies

It does not reflect well on you to talk negatively about companies on your resume. It's natural to have a few bad experiences, but be sure to paint them in the right light. If you talk negatively about a previous company, it implies that you will talk negatively about the company you're interviewing for now in the future. I've seen CEO's reject candidates at the last minute because of this.

Don't come under-dressed

This is a sensitive one. It's hard to know exactly what to wear. Overdressing typically means wearing a suit. Use your judgment, of course but always lean toward overdressing. 75% interviewers have said that most candidates turn up dressed shabbily or inappropriately for an interview. Follow the above attire checklist for creating a great impression.

Cursing

Please watch your language. Cursing implies that you don't communicate professionally in the workplace.

Conclusion

I believe the content of this book is very insightful. It has enlightened you on uncommon truths that are helpful in getting a job. Numerous people across the globe who have been unemployed for many years after graduating from tertiary institutions would have been enjoying better, happier and more prosperous lives as employees if they had access to the information in this book while they were fresh graduates. Numerous fresh graduates would unarguably get good jobs (even faster than they think) if they digest the content of this book and allow it to guide their job search activities.

You are very fortunate if you came across this book as a fresh graduate, as long as you will apply the principles it recommends in your job search activities. This book will save you years you would have wasted searching for jobs. It will also help you to make the best out of job opportunities you will come across, some of which you would have wasted. You are also very fortunate if you come across this book as a worker (and you are willing to be guided by its content) because it can help you get a better job, if you desire such. This book simplifies how to get a job. It enlightens the reader on what employers want from job seekers. It is a very reliable and authoritative manual for job seekers.

In competing for limited job opportunities, I am very confident that the job seeker who has undergone training in recruitment education has higher chances of getting a job than his competitors, even those who are more intelligent than he is, but lack recruitment education. The ideas that were exposed in this book have no place in the school curriculum (from the least to the highest level). As a matter of fact, I am very fanatical about the limitations of the educational system in its present form. The type of education that is offered to students in conventional schools does not adequately prepare them for real life challenges (after graduation).

This is one of the reasons most graduates have difficulties meeting real life challenges after numerous years of leaving school. This is why I recommend Supplementary Education to every graduate. Ideally, supplementary education ought to have a place in the school curriculum to assist students to be more focused and productive when school days are over. Most unfortunately, it does not. This shows that much of what students are taught in school are things they do not need to succeed in real life. By this token, most of what students need to survive in the real life are not taught in the school. I once argued that

"An uncommon truth among most graduates is that most of what they need to know in order to achieve a bright future are things that are not taught in school. This, however, is not a way of discrediting the value of education. The society cannot do without school. The school system produces professionals the society cannot do without. Your years in school should not be considered a waste of time and resources. The point being made is that what you learnt in school is inadequate for your success. The deficiencies of the school system make room for Supplementary Education. Supplementary Education is complementary, auxiliary and ancillary education. You will have no meaningful success in the future, even as a graduate, if you lack this type of education, no matter your course of study, your grade or the school you attended."

As noted above, it is impossible to have any meaningful success in the real life (i.e. life after school) in the absence of supplementary education. The major factor that underlies the failure of most graduates in real life is the absence of supplementary education. This highlights the necessity of this type of education. As seen above, one of the reasons many graduates remain unemployed after years of leaving school, despite being exceptionally intelligent, is that they lack Recruitment Education. They are ignorant of what employers want from job seekers. They are ignorant of what they need to know in order to be able to convince prospective employers that they are the best candidates for the positions they applied for.

This book in your hand is aimed at providing you with one of the supplementary education you need. This is, perhaps, the first type of supplementary education you need to succeed in the real life. It is called Recruitment Education. It is an education that prepares you for getting a job, if not for getting your dream job. This is the aspect of life's challenges it is geared towards addressing. There are other types supplementary education which are geared towards addressing the challenges in other areas/aspects of life. Since success is essentially concerned with striving for balance in all areas of life, this supplementary education is inevitable for everyone, even non graduates, who sincerely and conscientiously desires to achieve a meaningful and successful life.

HOW TO ANSWER INTERVIEW QUESTIONS

Guide to a Winning Interview with Amazing Interview Answers. How to Use Emotional Intelligence to be More Confident in your Job Interview.

Jim Hunting

Introduction

When attending an interview, you need to show your assertiveness, you have to practice being confident. Often, confidence starts with the mindset that you can accomplish all things on your agenda. Being more assertive starts with being proactive about your own life. When you think about what you want to do, then you can set a goal and do it faithfully. That means practicing what you preach. You have to try to do your best at what you do, because then you can be confident. It all starts with being excellent at what you do. However, even then, you can develop confidence when your skill is not the best.

Begin by getting good at what you do

One thing that you have to do is be good at what you do. That will be the first step to a successful interview process. You cannot succeed in securing a good job if you're not good at what you do. Even if you do succeed at the interview, you won't last long, if you're not skilled at the job that you want to do. Therefore, it is crucial that you find ways of developing your talent and tailoring your skills to your job. Then, you can have the qualifications necessary to get the job that you want.

Get qualified and get the education you need

The next step is getting qualified. Go and get that certificate. Get the credentials that you need to confidently submit your resume to the place where you want to work. You will need these things, because when you talk about your experience, then you can bring them up at the interview. Get as many qualifications as you can, because these will enable you to get the interview, and you'll be able to support your candidacy. The more qualified you are, the more confident you will be.

Emphasize your strong points but don't gloss over your weaknesses

Now that you are qualified, you should try to emphasize the strong points in your life that you have. Write down all your strengths on a piece of paper, and expand on each of them. Consider them deeply and think about what makes you great at what you do. Then, you can talk about your weaknesses. For every weak point that you have, try to come up with ways that you are handling these weaknesses. Think of ways you're improving yourself or finding ways to get more training and support to help you along the way. It will show some humility and the fact that you want to continually advance in your life.

Do some breathing exercises

Another thing that you should do is some deep breathing. Try to take in as much oxygen as possible before and during the interview. It is important that you are breathing a lot, because that will help you feel better. Also, if you can focus on one thing, it should be breathing in a healthy way. Try doing this, and you should notice how your nerves simply melt away.

Be positive

Believe that you deserve and are meant to be at the place where you're going to. You should show confidence, and by being positive and having a good mindset, then you'll be ready to show that you know your stuff in the interview. The important thing is to keep your chin up and keep going, even when your body is fighting and making it difficult to function while you're in the interview.

Don't fidget during the interview

Avoid making fidgety movements during the interview, which could show that you are very nervous and could make it more difficult for you. Try to remain as stationary as possible in your seat so you don't make any involuntary movements. Be conscious of your posture at all times, and keep your feet planted in front of you.

Press the pause button

Another thing that you need to do is press the pause button when you feel like you're going to veer off course. Let's say you're answering a question, and you have to talk about your previous job experience and how it was. You don't want to go off endlessly in the wrong direction about it. If you hit the pause button, then you can stop yourself from answering a question in too much detail. To answer a question succinctly and fully, you should try to say what is needed without including any additional information. Stop yourself from going any further.

Chapter 1: Before the Interview

1. Research the Backgrounds of the Interviewers*

The company you are interviewing with will typically send over the interview schedule in advance. If there are multiple rounds of interviews, you may only interview with one person the first round and then with multiple people in subsequent rounds.

It is essential to know some background details about each person who interviews you. Each interview usually begins with small talk to break the ice. Having knowledge of the interviewer's professional background goes a long way in building rapport early on. It is also an excellent way to develop relevant questions for the interviewer at the end of the session (See tip #2 for more detail).

I recommend starting your research with the company's website. If it is a small to mid-size company, you will usually come across profiles of the leadership team. Larger companies do not always publish leadership profiles. If you are unable to find the profile of your interviewer on the company's site, LinkedIn will be an excellent resource. Within each LinkedIn profile, you will find "Experience," "Skills & Endorsements," and "Activity" which will include articles or posts made by that individual to their network. There is also an "Interests" section which will show which companies and organizations that person is connected to. Reviewing the interests section is a great way to find clues about which causes and charities they focus on outside of work. I do not recommend making a "Connect" request to your interviewers on LinkedIn before the interview. They may not recognize who you are beforehand, and it is a much more natural progression to make the request after meeting them during the interview.

You can also conduct a Google search to look for articles and information on your interviewer. You will often find local news articles about business leaders getting involved in community and charitable events.

As you are conducting research on your interviewers, jot down bullet points of relevant information that you can leverage during your interview. Here is an example of what your notes might look like:

Jim Vandenberg, Director of Procurement

- Attended University of Michigan (From the dates, I'm noting that he attended when they won the 1997 national championship in football).
- Manages a team of 21 professionals responsible for sourcing raw materials, warehousing, suppliers, and logistics.
- Started career in corporate finance.
- Interested in St. Jude's Children hospital.

Possessing this background information on Jim gives you a huge advantage for the interview! The key is not to lead with any of this information but to naturally incorporate it into your conversation and leverage it to ask excellent questions. For example, you would never want to say something like:

"I saw that you were attending Michigan in 1997, did you attend any games the year the football team won the championship?"

Or

"I noted that you follow St. Jude's Hospital. What other charitable organizations interest you?"

These questions would be coming out of left field and scream to the interviewer that you investigated them. Instead, use this information during the natural progression of the conversation. For example, the interviewer will typically tell you some of their background information in the beginning. If the interview is still in the "small talk" phase and Jim stated that he attended the University of Michigan, you can say something like:

"I'm always thrilled when fall comes along and it's time for college football season. Michigan has such a rich history in football. Did they have good teams while you attended?"

You can be assured that 99 out of 100 times, Jim is going to light up like a Christmas tree and tell you about being on campus when they won the national championship. This will get him excited to discuss it with you and the interview starts out in a positive direction. If football (or whatever background information you found on the interviewer) is not your thing, do not sweat it. You certainly do not want to use the above example if you have no interest in football. However, you should be able to find something else in their background that you can relate to and bring it up when the time is right.

At the end of the interview Jim is going to ask if you have any questions. Since you researched his background information, you can ask him some excellent questions you come up with in advance such as:

"As the director of procurement, how do you take steps to mitigate the risk of large or unexpected price movements in raw materials?"

"Does XYZ Company offer employees the opportunity to get exposure working with multiple departments?"

"Does XYZ Company encourage employees to give back through charitable causes?"

Notice how each question is driven by background information from the notes above? They are also highly relevant questions that Jim will be eager to discuss.

You can certainly come to the interview with relevant questions that are not rooted in an interviewer's background information, but most candidates struggle to come up with two or three strong questions for each interviewer. Leveraging their background information is an excellent way to formulate them.

2. Develop Questions for Each Interviewer*

One of the most critical parts of the interview is towards the end when the interviewer will ask you if you have any questions for them. Not only do they expect you to ask questions, they also expect the questions to show that you did your research on the company and are genuinely excited about the position.

Candidates should be ready to ask each interviewer a minimum of 2 questions, but I always recommend having 3 questions prepared. When coming up with your questions, be sure to avoid any question that can be answered with a simple "yes" or "no" response. For example:
"Does XYZ Company offer paid leave for new fathers?"

Even though this question will probably not result in the interviewer providing a simple "yes" or "no," it is possible to be answered with a one-word response and is usually not relevant to the interview. In fact, the interviewer may not even know the answer to this question which would disrupt the flow of the conversation. This type of question should be saved for your HR contact after they offer you the job.

Your questions should be broad enough to get the interviewer thinking but specific enough to their background and role that they are enthusiastic about answering them. This is too broad of a question:

"What do employees enjoy about working at XYZ Company?"

Instead be more specific to the interviewer's role and show you did some research with this question:

"As someone who works closely with a wide range of customers in the consumer products industry, where do you look for opportunities to bring added value to your customers?"

The best way to develop highly relevant questions for each interviewer is to research their background and experience (see tip 1). Below are a couple more examples of taking notes on your research to create high quality questions.

Nicole Bennet, Accounting Manager

- Attended University of Utah, was in Beta Alpha Psi (accounting group).
- Spent time in public accounting at a Big Four Firm (PwC).
- Is responsible for overseeing quarterly and annual financial reporting with SEC and coordination of audit with independent accounting firm.
- Interested in hiking and outdoors groups.

Question 1: "What role does technology have on the challenges and opportunities facing the financial reporting profession as it relates to SEC reporting?"

Question 2: "How do you leverage student organizations on college campuses in your recruiting efforts?"

Question 3: "How does XYZ Company encourage employees to be active and participate in fitness activities?"

Kelvin Smith, Regional Sales Manager Software company

- Lives in Chicago, responsible for all Midwest sales.

- Previously was a recruiter for sales positions.
- Oversees large sales team with customers primarily in automotive manufacturing.
- Interested in Veteran Affairs and supporting VA hospitals.

Question 1: "How does your team leverage CRM (customer relationship management) technology to bring value to your customers?"

Question 2: "With software and technology changing so rapidly, how does your sales team work with the operations and technology teams to leverage customer feedback and interaction?"

Question 3: "How does XYZ Company and its employees give back to charities, veterans causes, and the local community?"

It can be challenging to remember all of your questions if you will be interviewing with multiple people. Be sure to jot them down under the name of each interviewer and bring them with you. You will typically have a brief break between interviews which will afford you the time to review them. You should usually avoid glancing down at them during the interview but just having them there will aid your confidence.

3. Ask the Interview Contact What Type of Interview to Expect

The style of the interview is dependent on the company's preference. Most companies prefer a traditional style interview where the candidate meets individually with the interviewers in separate sessions. However, some companies will conduct other types of interviews including:

*Panel interviews where multiple people observe the interview session and take turns asking the candidate questions.

*Presentation interviews where the candidate is expected to put together a presentation and present it to a group of interviewers.

*Brain teasers or test type interviews where the candidate has a fixed amount of time to complete a competency test to assess knowledge and critical thinking skills.

Some interviews are set up as a combination of the types listed above. For example, the candidate may be asked to complete a 30-minute competency test before commencing a more traditional one-on-one interview session. Regardless of the type of interview coming your way, you can be fully prepared to succeed. However, it is essential to know what type of interview to prepare for as soon as possible.

The type of interview can usually be determined by the schedule or itinerary sent over. If the company does expect you to give a presentation, they will let you know up-front. If the schedule shows you meeting with various individuals in interview sessions, you can expect to have a more traditional style interview. If your schedule only shows the beginning and end times of the interview, be sure to reach out to your contact and ask them what to expect. Being mentally prepared for one-on-one interview sessions is much different than interviewing in front of a multi-person panel. When asking what to expect, be sure not to phrase it in a way that insinuates you are looking for tips or inside information about the process. Instead, emphasize that you would like to know what to expect to help you prepare for the interview. Here is an example email you could use to send to your HR contact:

"Hi (first name),

I am looking forward to interviewing with XYZ Company on mm/dd (date). As I am starting to prepare for the interview, I wanted to reach out to you with a few questions that came up.

Should I expect the interview to be conducted in multiple sessions or will I be interviewing in front of a panel of people?

If possible, could you please provide me with the names of the people who will be included in the interview process?

Should I bring a calculator or pencils for any testing procedures?

Once again, I greatly appreciate the opportunity to interview with XYZ.

Thank you,

(your first name)

4. Take Note of the Company's "About Us" Information

Companies will almost always have a section on their website that discusses their values, culture, mission statement, history, and objectives. By absorbing this information, you will have a great sense of what they tend to look for in candidates. Many studies show that companies place a higher emphasis on cultural fit than any other trait when deciding whether to hire a candidate.

It is not uncommon for an interviewer to test a candidate on their knowledge of the company's values. They may ask the candidate which values they look for in an employer to see how well they align with the company's values. You can use the information obtained in your research to emphasize key values of your own that match up well with those of the company.

I do want to emphasize that you should not waste time memorizing everything on the company's "about us" section. It is more important to take bullet point notes of their values, mission, and culture. You can use that information to think of ways to emphasize your own values and interests that closely align with those of the company. If a company's values include the following terms:

*Integrity

*Accountability

*Diversity

*Quality

You should find ways to integrate some of these values into your answers to the interview questions. For example, if the interviewer asks you to provide them with an example of a time you faced a tight deadline on a project and in part of your answer you say, "I always place a high emphasis on quality, no matter what type of pressure I face," you have successfully aligned your answer with one of the company's values and the interviewer will usually make that connection.

5. Use Twitter/Facebook/LinkedIn to Research the Company's Personality

Social media is an excellent way to learn about the culture and atmosphere within a company. Companies will usually post news articles, press releases, updates, and engage with their audience on their social media page. Reviewing this activity on social media will give you a strong sense of their culture and tone. Is the tone they use on their social media pages very professional or is it more laid back and casual? Do they only self-promote on their pages or do they find other ways to engage with their audience? What positive news and information are they sharing with their audience?

Within a few minutes of reviewing their social media activity, you will get a strong sense of the company's culture and personality. This will usually be an indicator of the style of the interview. It may be serious and professional or more laid back and casual. You will not know for sure until the interview takes place but their activity on social media will provide a lot of clues. If any exciting updates or news articles shared by the company catch your attention, be sure to take note of them and you can bring them up during the small talk phase of the interview or even turn them into a question for the interviewer.

Chapter 2: The Power of
The First Handshake

Never underestimate the power of a handshake. Handshakes are a symbol of goodwill and agreement, but it can also be used to send a strong subliminal message of authority.

There are three kinds of handshakes.

The dominant handshake that uses the palm-facing downwards to create an impression of authority. Use the dominant handshake in meetings that have a crucial agenda where the decision will either benefit or damage your firm.

While, the submissive handshake delivers the opposite message with the palm faced upward. It is never recommended to use the submissive handshake because you need to lead people and not the other way around.

And the standard handshake creates a sense of equality between two people by making both hands hold in the same manner. Make a standard handshake when you meet customers and clients to imply that you are both in the same level. This also helps make you appear approachable to people. After sealing a deal, use the standard handshake again to send a message of satisfaction.

Make your handshakes firm and warm. A firm handshake is a sign of confidence and power. In the US, women shake their hands only by holding the edge of the fingers. However, women in business don't. They still prefer the classic business shake. Holding on to the edge of the hand will make people think that their hands are dirty or you don't like them at all.

Time the handshakes well. Simply hold and pump the hands three times in an up-down motion. You can further reinforce friendship by using the other hand to slightly hold the shoulder, elbow or forearm of your partner. Finally, while you shake hands, make it sincere by brightly smiling at them. Although handshakes are a small gesture that happens only in 5 seconds, it creates positive energy both at the beginning and ending of meetings.

Establish authority with non-verbal communication

In the business world, not only do we need to create trust, we also need to build authority. Our behavior during a meeting speaks a lot about how credible and confident we are. A good show of body language can affect your sales and even job position.

Your posture and height are the one of the few things that people notice. People who are tall and stand straight are associated as being confident. This is highly important in business especially when dealing with clients. Posture creates positive energy that you are not burdened with problems. Straight posture can further add authority if your chin is slightly pointing upward and your chest is projected outward.

People get influenced easily if you speak to them while looking in their eyes. This conveys an image of seriousness and adds credibility to your message. Be mindful that you should look in a person's eyes only 60% of the time. Any more than this will intimidate your client. Use the other 40% looking at random areas beside the eye to ease tension.

While walking exude confidence and authority by swinging your arms in a firm manner. Make every action precise. Eloquence while moving make it appear that you don't make mistakes and that you calculate every movement.

Previously, we discussed the Merkel Rhombus, which is a hand gesture created by holding your hands together and forming a triangle, and then slightly moving the thumbs toward you to make a rhombus shape. The Merkel Rhombus is a new gesture that symbolizes a calm but serious behavior. Using this body language will make you approachable at the same time respected.

The Merkel Rhombus goes well with a firm and soft voice. People tend to listen more closely to a soft but audible voice rather than a loud one. A slow rhythm will make every person cling on to your every word. Just be careful not to speak too slowly because people might lose interest in you.

While standing up, take note of your feet. You might be appearing confident from the waist up, but if your legs won't lose their nerves, they'll make it obvious. Counter this by slightly opening your legs and creating a 45 degree angle between them. Refrain from moving because it might bring back your anxiety and soon you'll be shaking again.

Contrary to popular belief, putting your hands on your waist is not a sign of felinity. In fact, male executives do this gesture more than women, for you make it appear that you are calm and relaxed in the face of stressful activities.

Combining these non-verbal authoritative cues to gestures that establish rapport will help you become an effective businessman. Non-verbal communication greatly increases your charisma that persuades people to agree to you.

Chapter 3: Questions About Your History

After they get a good sense of who you are inherently, they are going to start to pull information from you to determine what experience you have. If you are a good person with a good head on your shoulders and have a good sense of responsibility, then of course, you've already passed the first part of the interview. The thing is, just being a good person doesn't mean you are always the right candidate for the job.

These types of questions will help them to see your history, what kind of educational experiences that you have, and what skills and lessons from your last job you will bring into this one. These are questions that will give the person conducting the interview the greatest sense of the type of employee that you would be.

"Why did you leave your last position?"

Now this is the juicy part, where you start to reveal all the reasons that you are here. The employer is asking you this because they want to know why things didn't work out. Was the other position just not right for you? Did you leave your last job for a similar reason that you might end up leaving this job at this company you are trying to work at? They're going to want to know what happened to get a better insight into what went on. Spare them the dramatic details and keep it professional.

"I left my last position because I felt as though there was no room for advancement. I lacked creative control and I felt that my voice wasn't being heard. I needed a positive change in my life because I want to continue to grow and move forward."

"How did you find out about this current position?"

The reason that employers might want to know this is because it will reveal even more about you. First, they are going to want to know if you know anyone that already works there. This gives them a personal recommendation which can be helpful in understanding who you are. They are also going to want to know if you were actively job-hunting and being proactive about finding a new position, or if this is just something that slipped into your lap. They are also going to be interested in figuring out if any of their marketing tactics to reach out to other potential candidates are working or not.

"I actually found a listing for this job on an online job board. I have been looking and applying to several places and the objectives and job description of this position intrigued me."

"Can you tell me about a time where you went above and beyond and did even more than what you were expected to do?"

This is a hard question because it will put you on the spot. Employers still want to see if you can come up with information like this quickly and without another prompt. Though challenging, you will still want to have a specific example so that they can truly see the nature of your character. You will want to pull preferably from a time period when you were working somewhere else. Don't lie and make yourself sound extra good – they will be able to tell. Be honest and speak from experience because it will be easier to remember this event when it comes time to talk about it then. Describe not just how you were able to go beyond what you were asked to do, but how you also managed to help the business out in some way as well. This would be a good answer, but remember to keep it specific to the scenario and not to base it verbatim of ours:

"There was a time when I used to work at the ice cream store in my hometown. At night, it would be our duty to clean the place up and then clock out. The morning staff would be responsible for setting up for the next day. One night we were rather slow, so I decided to do all of the morning prep. The next day, the workers came in and didn't have to do much at all, making their morning start off easier. On top of that, they were able to open early and let some people in the store who had already been waiting."

"How would your last boss, manager, or supervisor describe you as an employee?"

This is another great question that they will likely ask you in some form or other. They want to know not just what you are like as an employee, but as someone who takes orders from the higher-ups. Were you feared by them? Did they have trouble telling you things? Were they your best friend? This previous relationship with the higher-ups will be important in helping them see what benefits you might bring to the position as an employee.

"I would say that I had a pretty good relationship with my last supervisor. We had open communication and instead of her always telling me what to do, we worked together to delegate tasks that I was better at to me and delegate tasks that she was better at to her, always checking in with each other to make sure both of our needs were being met."

"Can you describe to me a time in the past at a different position in which you were faced with a very challenging scenario, and what you did in the moment to resolve the issue?"

This is a good question where your answer will show that you are recognizing what you might have struggled with in the past, and how you handle pressure when you are faced with an obstacle. Remember to stay honest, and don't feel the need to go into every last agonizing detail about this.

"There was a time when I worked retail at a small gift shop. I noticed that a woman was stuffing some smaller jewelry pieces into her purse. She was standing right by the door, so I feared that she was going to make a run for it. I asked her if she needed any help and showed her some merchandise at the back of the store to buy me time while I talked to the owner. She was about to leave when I asked her if she was going to pay for the items in her purse. After retrieving the items, the owner and I decided to let her go since it was less than $30 worth of merchandise, but we made sure she wasn't allowed back in. I panicked at first and wanted to stop her immediately, but that could have turned into a messy situation, so I tried to remain as calm as possible and work with my supervisor to find the right solution."

"What is something that you saw a different employee do that you wouldn't do yourself? Can you describe a time when a coworker did something they shouldn't do? How did you handle this?"

This question might be phrased in a few different ways, but it's an important one that will give them insight into what you believe a good employee should be like. There are a ton of employees who do the wrong thing, so when you can show that you recognize the difference between right and wrong, it makes you all the more trustworthy. Don't shame anyone, don't use names, and make sure that you aren't being rude. Simply state what they did wrong, why it was wrong, and how you would have corrected the situation. Here is an example:

"There was a time in my last job when my coworker would always leave her leftover tasks for the person that came into the next shift. Even though she worked a slower shift, there would still be leftover tasks that she didn't bother to complete. Initially, I confronted her about it. I made sure all my tasks were done and left a note asking to help out during the slow shifts since ours were busier at night. She ended up ignoring this, so I had a discussion with my boss, and we came up with the perfect task list that fairly delegated the right amount of duties."

"What was the best part about your last position?"

This is a question that will let your interviewer know what you value the most in the workplace. When you can discuss with them the benefits of a position, they will be more likely to see what things you are passionate about. Be honest with this, but of course keep it professional. You might have enjoyed that you had a few hours a day to sit on your phone after the boss went home, or maybe you liked that you got a free meal every shift. Keep it professional. Say something like this:

"One of the best parts of my last job was the sense of community that was there. Everyone got along and we all managed to work together in a harmonious way, playing off each other's strengths and weaknesses. It was unfortunate when I had to leave, but luckily, I still keep in contact with many of the same people and have no issue including them in my life to this day."

"If you were in a position where you had to fire someone, how would you do it? Have you ever had to let someone go in the past? What is your method for doing so?"

Not every position that you are interviewing for is going to require you to have to fire someone. There might still come a time when you have to be a part of the process of letting someone go. This is a challenging scenario that requires someone empathy, but also strong enough to reveal the truth. Even if you don't think you'd ever be in that position for the job that you are interviewing for, it's still important to have an answer to this question. Start by saying something such as this:

"I never have had to do this in the past, but I would imagine it would be a difficult scenario. If I ever had to, I would start by ensuring that I am in a private room with the person so as not to embarrass them. I would let them know the reason there is an issue in the first place, and then gently reveal to them what is going to happen next. I'd give them the remainder of the day to clear out if they wanted to but give them the freedom to decide when to leave during the day."

"What has been your greatest achievement in life? What about in your career?"

This question is usually asked because they want to know what your biggest accomplishment is. Think about what has been the single most important time in your life or something that you are proud of to share with others. They want to see your passion as you talk and find out how you might have been able to improve your own life.

Make sure that when you share this you give a personal or a career related answer, depending on how they might end up asking.

"My greatest achievement was certainly getting my Master's degree. Before I even applied to graduate school, I was nervous. I thought I wouldn't be able to do well because I had a bad semester as an undergrad. I let this become my source of motivation and graduated at the top of my class! Whenever I doubt myself I don't use my degree as a reminder, but instead, my dedication that was required for all the hours of studying and homework to remind me of all the things that I'm capable of."

Chapter 4: Talking About Your Advantages And Disadvantages

"Tell us about your pros and cons" - this is probably one of the most common questions in the interview. Someone is offered to name three of their weaknesses and three strengths, others are asked to describe the personality traits that hinder or help them in building a career – there are a plenty of options how recruiters formulate this question.

First, let's understand why this issue consistently ranks among the most frequently asked during the interview. What recruiters want to hear from the candidates? Honest confession of laziness and lack of organization or pompous speech of "I have virtually no weaknesses"?

Neither one nor the other. By asking the applicant about his advantages and disadvantages, a specialist of recruitment wants to know how mature is a person sitting in front of him, what is his self-esteem, if he is able to work constructively, including on himself. as it is known, there are no people without flaws: we are all woven of good and bad qualities. Namely in their recognition psychologists tend to see a sign of a stable and mature personality.

However, you do not need to invent anything to show recruiters that you fully meet the job requirements. Lying at the interview will not help you make a career. Be honest, but think over your answer in view of the given recommendations:

Lows in the pros. Psychologists believe that the best practice is response to a question about the shortcomings at the interview indirectly pointing out own advantages. "Friends think I'm meticulous. I really scrupulous, like checking all the details, and it annoys people. But I'm trying to learn to look at things more widely," – this is an excellent response of the applicant applying for the position of design engineer. "I think I am over-talkative, perhaps this is a consequence of my profession" - a good option for a candidate for the position of PR-manager or marketing specialist.

Another option of answer to the question about the shortcomings is to mention the lack of professional knowledge, not directly related to the desired position. Thus, you will demonstrate your recruiters frankness and willingness to develop. For example, if you are applying for a position of news feed reporter, you can safely admit that so far have not mastered the genre of the essay: in this work, you likely will not need this skill in the near future. However, you should still be careful not to harm yourself - think carefully about the answer.

Think about how the qualities which you are going to tell recruiters will create for you a competitive advantage over other candidates. For example, do not point to your leadership skills where they are not needed. "I'm pretty ambitious," - says the candidate for the post of accountant in a company with an established structure and ... left without a job offer. But in the young company, vigorously seizing market, such quality may well come in handy.

How to answer personal questions during the interview?

In preparation for the interview, many job seekers think through in advance the answers to possible questions - about the professional accomplishments, the reasons for leaving previous job, career goals. But personal questions are often taken by surprise. What recruiters want to know, asking, for example, about the reasons for divorce or the presence of chronic diseases in the child? How to respond to such questions, and whether to do it?

In most cases, questions about the private life are not caused by idle curiosity of recruiters; they have very specific goal - a more or less accurate psychological profile of the candidate. Experienced hiring managers know that often information which, at first glance, is not related to the professional qualities of the applicant, says more about him than he was talking about himself. That is why many HRs go for a violation of ethical norms and show interest to the private life of the candidate.

For the successful employment psychologists advise not to neglect the possible answers to personal questions: "What you care about that?" "Why do you want to know?" - such counter-questions to address HR management hardly will benefit your career. Try to find an opportunity to respond, and if the question seems too personal, politely and gently turn the conversation in another direction.

"Do you live with parents or separately?" - it would seem, what does this have to do with future work in the position of sales manager? Meanwhile, detailed response to this question can talk about such personal characteristics of the applicant, as the maturity, independence, responsibility towards the family, as well as on the level of his income. If a candidate talks about high earnings in the previous place of work, but he lives in a studio apartment with his parents or other relatives, recruiter may begin to doubt his sincerity, and hence the level of professionalism.

"Do you have your own apartment or rent it?" – this is another frequent question during the interview. At first glance, what interest business recruiter has to jobseekers property? Most likely, in such way the personnel manager is trying to understand the structure of your costs. It's one thing if the candidate has his own housing, the other - if he is forced to save each month rather big amount to pay the rent of apartment, and the third - if he pays the mortgage. In addition, the answer to this question will help supplement your psychological portrait of valuable information - whether you are willing to bear a serious responsibility to the credit institution.

Many young women have heard on interview questions like, "When you are planning to have a baby?" Of course, this is a very personal question, and often job applicant lost in answering it. After all, it is not always possible to accurately plan the birth of a baby: it is a question not only of the desire but also the state of health.

Desire of recruiter to know about your plans is clear: not all employers are willing to invest in the adaptation of the employee, which soon plans to leave on maternity leave. How to answer this question - directly or evasive, you decide. "In the near future we do not plan to have children" – such a response do not oblige you to anything, and thus dispels some fears of employer.

By law, you cannot be refused to be accepted for a job if you want to become a mother, or are already pregnant. However, it is likely that the true cause of refusal in this case will not be communicated.

"How often your child is sick?" is one more personal question, often asked by women during the interview. At this, for recruiter it does not matter what the temperature accompanies a cold in a baby - he is more concerned about the frequency and duration of your sick lists. It is better to answer frankly, because it is important also for you: the HR manager asks you to prioritize. If the career for you at the moment is no less important than the education of offspring, boldly answer that there is someone to look after baby. "The child is sick as often as other children, but grandmother (nurse, husband, etc...) is ready to stay with him" - this answer is quite satisfactory for the employer.

"What are you fond of?", "Do you have any hobbies?" – asking such questions recruiters are trying to figure out what are your temperament and character, whether you are suitable for the position by personal qualities. If, for example, the candidate claims to PR-manager position in a young and rapidly growing company, but says that he spends weekends in a chair knitting, the manager on staff will have reasonable doubts in his sociability.

"What is the last book you read?" – this is a question for revealing the overall development of the candidate. What he reads - only professional literature or finds the time to reread the classics? Although the objectivity of this method could be argued, it is still applied. There is no need to compose a list of literature, which, as it seems to you, makes you smarter in the eyes of a hiring manager. It is better to call the two books that you really have read recently: one professional and one fiction. Thus, you show that you develop not only as a professional but also as a person.

Personal questions are not uncommon in the interviews, and how you respond to them, to some extent, the decision about accepting you in a new team depends on. Therefore, talking with recruiters, be polite, diplomatic and sincere. If you do not want to respond to some particularly personal question - calmly and kindly tell that you are not ready to discuss it.

Chapter 5: Power Words to Blow Them Out Of The Water

Your goal in an interview is to make an impression and stand out from the crowd. There are some words that you can use to do just that. Barry Drexler, an interview coach, has conducted more than 10,000 interviews, and with his experience in HR, he has come up with 12 of the most powerful words that you should use in the interview process.

Leadership and management

You may not be applying for a position as a manager, but many companies want to know that you have some experience in this area, because you may be called upon to lead a team or give orders in some capacity. Even Burger King has some supervisors. So, if you can say things like "I managed a team of workers or I led a group of colleagues," then you can have a leg up in the process, because you demonstrate that you have skills that can eventually lead to leadership opportunities, even within this company.

Strategy and plan

Employers view candidates who have a strategic plan in mind more favorably. If you have experience with roles or responsibilities that required strategy, it shows that you have a background that is necessary to take on challenges and difficulties that may come your way in your new role. If you have a plan, then you know what to do and what steps you need to take to achieve the goals and complete tasks that are required for the job function. It also shows that you are a visionary who will carry out a plan to completion.

Established

Drexler says this word is powerful, because it shows that you have been able to complete a project and it demonstrates your authorship of a strategy or plan that was carried out. For example, you could say that you established a certain plan for a company. That would carry a lot of weight, because you authored the plan that was completed and accomplished a goal for the company.

Results and achieved

Employers love it when you talk about what you have achieved. This shows that you were able to reach the objectives that you had set. It also shows that you are a committed employee who always follows through on promises, goals, and other objectives that are set. It also gives you a sense of credibility and proves you are trustworthy as a worker. It is powerful for the interviewer to hear about the goals you have achieved.

Influence

Another word that is important is influence. When you show that you have influenced others, then you show yourself to be both a reliable and interesting candidate. You can talk about how you influenced the management to carry out some kind of plan. Instead of saying, "My managers really liked my plan," you could say, "I influenced the management to carry out this action plan, which succeeded in growing the business."

Recommend and suggest

When you use these words, you show that you are willing to contribute to the growth of the organization and want to do your best to promote your own plans and persuade the management to follow your advice and ideas. For example, you could say, "I recommended that my boss do _____, and they listened to my counsel. In the end, the business succeeded in _____."

Collaborate

When you use the word "collaborate", you indicate that you can work well with others. You're not just working for yourself. Instead, you're proving that you can be a member of a team and contribute meaningfully to it. You can talk about how you collaborated with others and how you were a key member of a group. You could say something like, "I collaborated with the marketing team to produce a strategy that worked for the company."

Example

Isaac is in an interview to get the position of data analyst.

Isaac: As you can see on my resume, I collaborated with many members of the data analysis team at my previous job. We were able to accomplish numerous tasks which enabled the company to move forward.

Interviewer: Isaac, would you tell us about a time where you had to lead a team?

Isaac: Yes, in fact, I led a team last year. We analyzed a survey that had been carried out by Coca Cola, and we were able to accomplish a goal. I collaborated with the members of the team. We succeeded in _____. In addition, I recommended to my manager that we do _____. In the end, my recommendation helped the organization to achieve the aim of _____.

Isaac used several keywords that were powerful and would wield influence over the decision of the HR team. He used to "accomplish", "collaborate", "succeed", "achieve", and "recommend", all of which would be helpful in securing him the position on the team.

Conclusion

It is important that you find ways that you can become more confident during an interview. You can use some power words to get you going. Always remember to be positive and reflect on your past experience, emphasizing what you were able to take from each aspect of your background. Strengthen your case by talking about your accomplishments, how you overcame adversity, and the skills that you can bring to the position. The main thing is matching your skills and experience with the position and proving why you would be the best candidate for the job. You have to find persuasive ways to do that. It all starts with your language and the words you choose to project your image. Remember that you have all the background and skills necessary to do it. All you need to do now is to communicate it and make your case. Then, you can achieve your goal and snag your dream job!

Chapter 6: People Skills Questions

Employers don't just care if you can do the job—lots of people can. What they want to know is if you want to do the job (your motivation) and if you'll fit in with the rest of the people you need to deal with (your people skills) on the job.

For this reason, behavioral interviewing is very common, which means the interviewer will ask lots of nosy questions about your past behavior, believing there's no better way to predict your future actions than by hearing about your previous actions in similar situations. You may also encounter situational interviewing, in which you are asked hypothetical questions so the interviewer can see how you react in imaginary situations, which may or may not take place in this job.

Behavioral interviewing asks lots of questions about your past behavior, because of the belief that past actions are the best predictors of your future actions in similar situations. Situational interviewing poses hypothetical questions like "what if or "let's say" to see how you'd behave in possible situations.

What is your management style? Or: Give me an example of when you had to show good leadership. Or: Describe your leadership style or skills...

What the interviewer is asking/looking for: In most industries, the ability to manage people is considered important to advancement in your career. Because of this, the interviewer wants to know how you lead, plan, organize, and control things—the four main components of management.

Good answer: Think about times when you got things done with the help of other people—if not at work, then in your volunteer, leisure, or school activities. Then think about good bosses and bad bosses you've had and why they were good or bad. Perhaps your bad boss used to give you deadlines and then ask a week before the due date where the project was, or yell at you without explaining what you did wrong, or hog all the credit.

You learned by negative example that a good boss gives credit where it is due, communicates clearly, and is fair. In addition, criticism of your work should be constructive, pointing out what you did wrong and what you need to do to improve without attacking you personally. Your answer should reflect some of these good traits, and be ready to give an example or two from your experience.

Bad answer: Anything that shows you haven't managed people at all or thought about how you deal with them. Or that you display the hallmarks of a bad boss.

How do you motivate people you manage?

What the interviewer is asking/looking for: He or she wants to see you are generous with praise and credit for a job well done, and possess enough insight to know different people are motivated by different things, instead of following a cookie-cutter management approach.

Good answer: Show that you aim to inspire and teach the people you manage and respect their individual differences, instead of being an autocrat who issues orders with no explanation.

Bad answer: An answer that reveals you don't bother much about motivating your underlings—and as far as trying to understand their differences, forget it.

Tell me about your track record for promoting your staff...

I had a team of 12 sales people and 8 of them got promoted in the last two years.

What the interviewer is asking/looking for: The interviewer wants to know you have the "right stuff" in terms of identifying talented workers and helping develop their potential so they can contribute to the best of their ability to your organization.

Good answer: Having staffers who rise in your organization reflects well on you as a manager, so hopefully your success ratio in this area is good and you can give an example or two to prove it.

Bad answer: An answer that shows you never met an underling you liked enough to develop them, which does not reflect well on your skills as a manager.

5 years ago (as an assistant) he really wanted to leave the company but I managed to convince him not to do so – and now he is the operations manager.

What the interviewer is asking/looking for: He or she wants to see that you can spot talent and potential, and point out a flaw that can stand some improvement tactfully, without losing the employee.

Did you watch The Apprentice, the hit TV reality show where job-hunters compete for a top, well-paying spot in Donald Trump's company? Well, lessons from the series are being taught at top business schools nationwide, as MBA students study how the job-seekers learned to think on their feet, take risks, choose their team, and defend their actions. Some major lessons from The Apprentice include:

• Bosses want to hire people who are like others on their current team.

• Pay attention to what the boss says are his or her company values.

• You're always being interviewed.

• You have to fight to get the job.

• Show respect for your peers.

• All companies want team players who pitch in.

Good answer: Give an example that shows how you were able to smooth a diamond in the rough's edges, or clarify how to produce good results in your organization, to enable the employee to reach his or her potential.

Bad answer: An answer that shows you are not skilled at people-problem solving, and don't really know how to salvage a talented employee with a flaw or two.

Describe a time when a personal commitment interfered with a business crisis or last-minute meeting...

I had a last-minute meeting with the CEO and the same afternoon my son had a very important soccer game, so I asked my wife to record it with our camcorder. The next day me and my son watched the entire game at home (eating popcorn, hot-dog, things like that) and it was fun!

What the interviewer is asking/looking for: He or she wants to know if, when the going gets tough, you'll be running off to a personal appointment, or you can be counted on when your employer really needs you.

Good answer: Give an example of how you rescheduled your personal commitment, or arranged to have someone else handle it, to show how loyal you are when your employer is in a crunch.

Bad answer: A remark or nonverbal cue that shows resentment and/or incredulity that your employer may ever expect to come above your personal life in your list of priorities.

How did you get along with your last work team?

I worked well with my team and their different personalities.

What the interviewer is asking/looking for: Trust me, the interviewer does not want to hear the gory details about the ghastly coworkers you are forced to put up with, any more than hearing about your boss, the head ogre.

Good answer: Give an example of how the team pulled together to achieve a goal. Show that you are cooperative and pleasant as well as a good worker.

Bad answer: A litany of how lazy, incompetent, or mean-spirited your team members were, in contrast to you, a saint.

Lace your answers with "we" and "our," not just "I," to signify you are a team player who has the employer's interests at heart, not just your own.

Can you give an example of how you increased sales, saved money, saved time, or improved efficiency at your job?

I handled my workload more efficiently by holding calls and returning them at a certain time of day to give me uninterrupted working time.

What the interviewer is asking/looking for: These are an employer's major goals, so the interviewer wants to know if you've ever brought "added value" by making a meaningful contribution in any of these crucial areas.

Good answer: Tell the interviewer about any time you brought in new business or made a suggestion your employer acted on—a potential client to pitch, an advertising or publicity campaign you dreamed up that increased a client sales and led to more business with your firm, an employee you referred, researching a cheaper way to deliver a product you worked on.

Bad answer: You can't think of any time you demonstrated "added value" to your employer. Isn't it enough you come in 9 to 5 five days a week?

Substance versus style: Most employers want both. They want to know you can do the job well (substance) as well as act appropriately with people you have to deal with (style).

What would you describe as a good work environment?

It is where talent and hard work are recognized and rewarded.

What the interviewer is asking/looking for: He or she wants to feel a work atmosphere you can thrive in mirrors their own, and is eager to avoid a bad fit like a very laid-back person in a pressure-cooker environment, which you will feel impelled to quit at the first opportunity.

Good answer: If you have any idea from your research what the work environment is like at this employer, try to reflect it in your answer. If not, say something like an atmosphere where people are motivated to pull together to produce a quality product or service. Who can argue with you?

Bad answer: An environment that bears no resemblance whatsoever to the employer in question, which means your days there will probably be numbered or you will do your work perpetually disgruntled.

Constructive criticism points out what you did wrong and what you need to do to improve without attacking you personally (for example, by berating you as stupid or incompetent).

How do you handle rejection?

I don't take rejection personally, but as an abstract turn-down of a product or service I am representing.

What the interviewer is asking/looking for: Because rejection is a crucial part of any job in sales, which includes public relations, customer service, and telemarketing, the interviewer wants to make sure you are secure enough to bounce back after being rejected, instead of taking it personally and feeling miserable.

Good answer: Rejection often gives you helpful information about how to convince your next sales prospect or overcome the objection of your current prospect, thus increasing your success ratio.

Bad answer: Any clue that you are insecure and will act devastated, defensive, or nasty after rejection, which will interfere with doing your job well.

How would your coworkers describe you? Or: How would your supervisor describe you?

Enthusiasm, reliability, integrity, and being a team player.

What the interviewer is asking/looking for: This is a cagey way for the interviewer to find out what you're really like at work, in the words of coworkers and bosses.

Good answer: Hopefully they will have recognized some of your greatest strengths. Cite some strengths employers tend to admire.

Bad answer: Blurting out how coworkers and your supervisor see you unfairly, and how they are wrong.

How far do you want to rise (or see yourself rising) in our organization?

As far as my skills and the employer will allow.

What the interviewer is asking/looking for: He or she wants to gauge your level of ambition and future orientation. Giving them a sense of how motivated and goal-directed you are is more important than naming a specific job title.

Good answer: Obviously, your advancement will hinge both on your doing well and your accomplishments being recognized and rewarded by the employer, so try something noncommittal. If your goal is to head the department you would be joining, or become sales manager for a larger territory, say so.

Bad answer: Anything that shows you have given no thought to your future beyond the job you are applying for. On the other hand, saying "I want your job" generally is a bit too bold for most interviewers.

Summary

"People skills" are important, and by now the interviewer has a pretty good sense of how you get along with people, manage people, and cope with people when they're difficult.

You've now described your style with examples of how you've acted in the past, while he or she already knows your substance or qualifications. He or she also has a sense of what you think is a good work environment, if you've ever brought added value by increasing sales or saving money (which is dear to any employer's heart), as well as how far you want to go.

• Be prepared to give examples of how you handled past situations at work.

• Be prepared to describe how you are a team player who gets along with many different types of people.

• Be prepared to give examples of how you increased sales, saved money or time, or increased efficiency at work.

• You may be asked how you would handle hypothetical situations at work.

Chapter 7: Industry Related Questions

Tell me about a time when you went above and beyond expectations for a project or assignment.

Question Type:

Behavioral

Question Analysis:

One of the most common performance ratings for a hardworking and competent employee is "meets expectations" however, there will be opportunities when an employee should think outside of the box and go above and beyond the call of duty. Interviewers want to know that the candidate is willing to embrace these opportunities instead of shying away from them. You should discuss an example of a time when you identified an opportunity to exceed expectations and took advantage of it to bring value to your team or to a customer.

What to Avoid:

You should avoid opportunistic dialogue such as "I always exceed expectations." The interviewer will know this is not a realistic response. You should avoid examples that would be expected of any normal hard-working employee such as "I had a tight deadline coming up, so I worked 50 hours one week instead of my normal 40."

Example Response:

S/T: In my previous position as a web developer, I was assigned to a project to help a new customer integrate a payment processor for their ecommerce platform. As I was reviewing their website code, I noticed some unrelated HTML errors that were hurting their search engine optimization. I estimated that it would take me an extra twelve hours to fix the code, but I had no extra time in my schedule.

A: I explained the situation to my manager and asked for permission to do the work for the customer outside of my current work commitments. She was impressed that I took the initiative to bring additional value to a new customer at the expense of my evenings over the next week. I informed the customer about the errors and explained the SEO value it would bring if I corrected them.

R: Both my manager and our customer were appreciative that I was willing to work the extra hours at no additional charge to correct the issue for them. They ended up choosing our firm for a major project three months later and mentioned their earlier experience working with me as a deciding factor.

Tell me about a time you had to meet a tight deadline. What was the outcome?

Question Type:

Behavioral

Question Analysis:

The interviewer will ask this question to assess how well the candidate works under pressure and to see if they are willing to go the extra mile. You should provide an example of an unexpected situation that involved careful planning and required you to go above and beyond normal expectations.

What to Avoid:

You should avoid providing an example that is associated with a routine task such as "our monthly report was due the next day, but I had not started it yet" because you likely would have known about the deadline in advance, so it can appear as though it is only a tight deadline due to poor planning. Unless there was a significant unforeseen circumstance, you should also avoid discussing an example of a tight deadline which you or your team were not able to meet it.

Example Response:

S: In my previous role as a systems analyst, I lead a project to implement an EDI integration for a client's new procurement software.

T: Two weeks before the project deadline, the client informed us of a significant issue with their legacy software which was having a major impact on their day-to-day business. They asked if we could accelerate our timeline to deliver our project in five days. My manager and I discussed the situation and agreed to let the client know we would do everything we could to meet their new request.

A: I brought our team together to explain the situation and let them know that we would be focusing our time exclusively on this project to try to meet the accelerated deadline. I mapped out all remaining tasks on a whiteboard and we agreed on completion dates for each task over the next five days. I also scheduled daily update meetings to ensure we were staying on track and available to each other when issues came up.

T: We worked 14 hours per day over the next five days but through our collaboration and perseverance we completed the project on time. The client was extremely happy with results of the project and our manager gave each of us three extra vacation days for our hard work.

Tell me about a time you disagreed with your boss. How did you handle it?

Question Type:

Behavioral

Question Analysis:

The interviewer will use this question to assess how well the candidate handles a disagreement with someone in an authoritative position. The response will say a lot about the type of working relationship the candidate might have with a future boss. Your example should show that you have confidence in speaking candidly with your boss while still respecting their point of view and authority. You should try to think of a situation in which you disagreed with a situation but offered an alternative solution.

What to Avoid:

In your example, you should avoid personally criticizing your boss. This can raise a warning flag about your character. You should also avoid examples in which you raised the disagreement with your boss in the presence of other team members. Unless your boss encouraged feedback in a group setting, disagreements with those in authority should be handled in a one-on-one setting.

Example Response:

S: In a prior role as a procurement analyst, I was on a team that worked on procurement process efficiency through the measurement of purchasing history and inventory turnover trends. In an effort to add more reporting functionality to our purchasing history, our boss worked on a project to switch us over to a new software package.

T: Although the reporting functionality had improved, the new software did not integrate directly with our company's ERP system, so we were required to manually upload our purchase history which often took us hours to do.

A: I set up a meeting with my boss to explain my experience and concerns with the software. I first told him that I appreciated his hard work in seeking to find better reporting solutions. I then explained that I felt the benefits of the new software were outweighed by the time it took our team to manually add the purchasing history data which slowed down our analysis. As an alternative solution, I showed him documentation of research I had done on comparable software that could be integrated with our ERP system.

R: My boss was appreciative of me being upfront and honest about the change. He also thanked me for my research on the software solution I came up with and one month later we ended up switching over to it.

What do you like most about working in this industry?

Question Type:

Industry and Company Specific

Question Analysis:

The interviewer will ask this question for a couple reasons. First, a new hire is an investment for the company, so they want to validate the candidate's passion and long-term commitment to the industry. They will also use the question to see how well the response aligns with the duties of the job. When discussing your favorite aspects about the industry, be sure to highlight those that are highly relevant to the position.

What to Avoid:

You should avoid discussing characteristics that do not pertain to the position. For example, if you are interviewing for a marketing position and the job description desires competency in Adobe Photoshop, you would not want to express how much you love working with Affinity Photo (Mac competitor to Photoshop). You should also try not to be too vague in your response. "I love that I get to work with people" does not sound nearly as good as "I enjoy working directly with clients to diagnose their challenges and offer solutions that bring them a better return on investment on their advertising budgets."

Example Response:

The thing I enjoy most about offering software solutions in the sales industry is that no two days are ever the same. I have the opportunity to work with such a wide range of clients who possess diverse challenges and needs for their human resource systems. I take pleasure in fostering client relationships. To me, success looks like a client reaching out for help with confidence that I can solve their problem. Believe it or not, I also really enjoy the travel associated with this industry. I consider it an opportunity to be able to explore new cities while I am traveling to meet with current and prospective clients.

What was the most difficult decision you have made in the past year?

Question Type:

Behavioral

Question Analysis:

Candidates without management experience will often get tripped up over this question because they have not had to make what would traditionally be considered a difficult decision such as cutting a budget or laying off an employee. However, there are plenty of opportunities to discuss difficult decisions outside of management roles. The interviewer is looking for an answer that demonstrates rationale and strong problem-solving skills. You should discuss an example that shows your ability to weigh options and critically think through the situation before coming to the decision. Some examples of tough decisions include: reporting unethical behavior, providing a negative review for a co-worker, choosing a new vendor, and turning down a promotion.

What to Avoid:

You should avoid discussing personal decisions that are not relevant to the position such as "I decided to purchase my first home last year" or "three months ago, I decided it was time to break it off with my fiancé." The interviewer is looking for your decision-making capabilities in a professional setting. Your answer should include the result of your decision, so you should avoid examples where the decision lead to an unfavorable outcome.

Example Response:

S/T: In a previous role selling professional services for IT projects, I was offered a promotion to be our company's Midwest resource services manager. I was honored to be offered the promotion and asked my boss for a few days to consider it. The new position would have increased my responsibilities while offering a raise in pay. At the time, I was in critical stages of a few projects with my clients. I was also making inroads with prospective clients that would soon lead to new business. Before the promotion came up, I had a strong interest in exploring future opportunities within the company's marketing team which would be a change to a new department.

A: I set up a meeting with my boss to discuss my desire to remain in my current position as well as my inclination to find an opportunity in the marketing department for my next career move.

R: At first, he was a little surprised that I decided to turn down the promotion, but he agreed with me that I brought the most value to our clients by remaining in my current position. He thanked me for my honest assessment and connected me with a manager in the marketing department to discuss future opportunities.

What motivates you?

Question Type:

Ambition

Question Analysis:

Candidates often struggle with this question because it is so broad in nature. The interviewer is typically using the question to understand what type of work is encouraging and fulfilling to the candidate. Coming up with an answer does require some personal reflection but ultimately your response should be centered around positive results or characteristics in the professional setting. Ideally, your motivation comes from something that aligns well with the company's culture.

What to Avoid:

Some candidates see this as such a broad question that they answer it with personal examples such as "my husband and kids" or "my lake cottage" but the interviewer is typically looking for motivation from a professional perspective.

Example Response:

I am motivated by a team culture that encourages collaboration and innovation. When team members are encouraged to work together to change things for the better, it brings lasting value to the whole organization. There is nothing I like more than envisioning a better way to do something and seeing it come to life.

What do you like to do outside of work?

Question Type:

Background and Personality

Question Analysis:

This may seem like a "softball" question but the interviewer will be paying close attention to your response to see if you are a good fit for the company's culture. Employers look for candidates who make the most of their free time. Your answer should be focused on activities that benefit your own wellbeing and the wellbeing of others in the community.

What to Avoid:

You should avoid discussing activities that sound unprofessional such as "I enjoy drinking and tailgating every Saturday during football season" or "I play video games each night." You should also be careful not to provide a dry response that makes it sound like you have no hobbies. This can create a negative perception about your personality in the eyes of the interviewer.

Example Response:

I am an avid golfer and fly fisherman. I try to play at least one round of golf each week during the spring and summer and I just got back from a fly fishing trip in Yellowstone National Park. I also enjoy giving back to the local community.

What is your management style?

Question Type:

Background and Personality

Question Analysis:

This question is very common when interviewing for management or supervisor positions but may also come up for any role that requires some level of leadership capability. The interviewer wants to know if your management style would be effective for the position and align well with the company's leadership culture. You should focus your response on your leadership traits that would fit well within the company and bring value to the position.

What to Avoid:

You should avoid using absolute words to describe your management style such as "always," "never," or "must." For example, scheduling regular team meetings to encourage team discussion and collaboration is an excellent tactic but if you say, "whenever an issue arises, I always schedule a group meeting to collaborate until we find an answer," it sounds like you react the same way to every problem. You should discuss your style with an emphasis on being able to adapt to a specific situation or to the unique personality traits of your team members.

Example Response:

I believe that the most effective managers are capable of adapting their style to the unique traits of each team member to empower them to reach their full potential. My typical management style is to lead by example, use clear and concise communication, encourage collaboration, and provide constructive feedback. As I get to know my team members, I will often make adjustments to my style to help bring more value to the team. For example, I typically like to meet with each of my team members once per month to discuss their concerns and offer constructive feedback. Last year, I noticed that one of my new team members was second guessing her work which was causing her to fall behind on a project. I decided to adjust my meeting schedule with her to once per week, so I could offer her more regular feedback. I immediately started to see an increase in her confidence which lead to better efficiency in her work. Eventually, she felt comfortable enough to reduce our meeting schedule to once per month. She mentioned that the weekly feedback I offered was a key element in helping her build up her confidence on our team.

Why should we hire you over the other candidates?

Question Type:

Background and Personality

Question Analysis:

This question is almost identical to question #3 but when some candidates are asked to compare themselves to the other candidates, they feel a sense of pressure to oversell themselves to the point of sounding like a used car salesman. However, it is important to remember that you will typically not earn the job offer on a single "grand slam" response. It is earned over the course of a full interview. The interviewer will use this question to learn more about the candidate's strengths and any type of unique value they would bring to the position. You should focus your answer on your strengths that correspond well with the job requirements and try to discuss at least one unique trait that would be attractive to the company.

What to Avoid:

Even though the question invites you to do so, you should avoid making any assumptions about the other candidates such as "I would work harder than any of the other candidates." Negative statements about candidates you likely do not even know can come off as presumptuous and arrogant. Instead, you can acknowledge that you cannot speak for the other candidates, but you feel confident that you are the right fit for the position.

Example Response:

Well, I cannot speak with regard to the other candidates, but I can tell you why I am an excellent fit for the position. My experience leading the development of over 25 successful web applications has put me in a position to understand what it takes to strategize, plan, and execute any type of coding project. My experience leading teams has taught me strong organizational and motivational skills. Aside from my strong skillset that aligns with the position, I am always looking to bring added value to any process or project through innovation. I am never content with a system or process if there is a more effective or efficient way. I typically drive innovation by collaborating with both internal and external resources and by leveraging new technology.

Tell me about a time you set a challenging goal for yourself. How did you ensure that you achieved it?

Question Type:

Behavioral

Question Analysis:

The interviewer will use this question to get a better sense of the candidate's ambition and initiative. They also want to know the strength of the candidate's planning skills when faced with a difficult challenge. In your response, you should focus the discussion around the planning and analysis that enabled you to take calculated actions to achieve your goal.

What to Avoid:

If you have professional experience on your resume, you should typically avoid discussing personal goals such as "I set a goal to lose 50 pounds" or "my goal was to complete a marathon." Instead try to draw on a goal you achieved that relates to your profession. You should also avoid trivial goals such as "I set a goal to arrive at work by 8:30 AM each day."

Example Response:

S: In my previous role as an IT security analyst, I noted that all managers and directors in my department had the Certified Information Systems Security Professional (CISSP) certification in their email signature. I spoke with my manager and learned that the company highly encouraged the certification for IT employees who sought promotions and leadership opportunities.

T: I wanted to place myself in a position to be considered for growth opportunities in our department, so I set a personal goal to pass the

CISSP exam within three months. The exam is six hours long and covers eight different subjects, so I knew I would need to create and execute a detailed plan to achieve my goal.

A: Before I started studying for the exam, I reviewed the study materials and spoke with co-workers who had passed the exam to determine the expected number of study hours. I looked through my calendar for the next three months to identify study time outside of the working days and on weekends. After determining that I would need roughly 100 hours to study for the exam, I created a robust plan assigning sections of the preparation materials to each study session on my calendar.

R: It was a strenuous three months, but I remained focused on my end goal to ensure I stayed on task with my study plan. I ended up acing the exam and I accepted a promotion within our department later that year.

Chapter 8: Informational Interviews

Informational interviews are a means to gather information about some specific career field or job. You can conduct these interviews and ask the participants questions before choosing your career.

Advantages of Informational Interviews

Informational interviews are very useful because they help to:

- Narrow down your options

- Prepare you for a specific career

- Discover occupations that you didn't know existed or weren't familiar with

- Gain self confidence and experience when interviewing with professionals

- Discover the types of personalities that thrive in particular career fields

- Have realistic expectations related to employment in particular fields

- Obtain an accurate idea of the existing job market

- Expand your connections with professionals in the field of your choice

How to Start

Choose an Occupation

You should select one or more occupations that you wish to investigate. Decide what information you are interested in acquiring about them. Write down all of the questions you want to get answered.

As with other interviews, it is recommended that you read and gather as much information about the company or organization as you can before you go to the interview.

Identify the People to be Interviewed

You can contact anyone for this type of interview. Start with a list of those people you already know such as your fellow students, friends, neighbors, people who worked with you in the past, or your present coworkers and supervisors. You can visit the alumni office or career center of your college and get the names of those who are currently working in the fields you are interested in. You can approach your family members' acquaintances or public speakers for an interview. Organizational directories, professional organizations, and the yellow pages are some other good resources. Besides this, you can also call a company and ask to speak to someone who has a particular job title.

Conduct Research Before the Interview

In order to conduct an effective informational interview, you cannot go in blindly. It is essential to prepare beforehand. You must do research about various things such as the company, its products, and the person you are going to interview. If you know enough about the company, you will be able to ask in-depth questions related to the job and organization. This in turn will give you the confidence to communicate efficiently.

There are a number of benefits to doing research.

- You can ask more relevant and intelligent questions.

- You can respond more thoughtfully if the interviewee asks any questions.

- You will not waste time by asking questions that can be answered easily by doing some research.

Think about what you want to know about a particular occupation and then figure out the people who may be able to provide that type of information. You can ask the organizations for their pamphlets and brochures to get additional information. The college's library can also be useful for this purpose.

Schedule the Interview

You can contact the person you want to interview in several different ways. You may send a letter or an email, make a phone call, or meet the person personally. You can even ask an acquaintance of the interviewee to get you an appointment.

Letter or Email

You can write an introductory email or letter similar to a cover letter that does not include a job pitch. It can be typed or printed neatly. It must include:

- A short introduction about yourself

- Your purpose for writing to the person

- A brief description of your interest or experience in the individual's field, location, or organization

- Why you wish to talk with the person

- Be straightforward and say you are seeking advice and information

- When and how you will be contacting the person again

Proofread and save the copies of all of the correspondence. Make it a point to contact them again as mentioned. You can call the person on phone and get an appointment. Do not wait for the prospective interviewee to call you on his own. If you are unable to contact the person, you can find out the most suitable time from the receptionist and call again.

Phone or in Person

People who participate in informational interviews usually allot around twenty to thirty minutes to talk about their professional expertise. You should be flexible about scheduling the interview because these interviewees have other commitments. In case a particular volunteer interviewee is too busy, ask him when you can call back and discuss setting up an appointment. Different techniques can be used to request an informational interview. Some good approaches are:

"Hello, I am so and so. I am doing career research related to your occupation. I would like to meet with you and talk to you for around thirty minutes to learn more about this particular job."

"Hi, I am so and so. I am studying at ABC college. I found your name in the organization's directory. I am interested in one day working in a career similar to yours. I hope you can help me to learn more about the job and career options. I would be delighted if you could spare twenty to thirty minutes for an informational interview."

If you want to personally ask the person for an appointment but are unable to meet with him, you can use the receptionists and other support staff as a resource to get information. You can ask them your questions because they may know a lot about the company.

They may be able to tell you how the company works and the job requirements and also name the key people. You should explain to them what you are seeking so that if they feel someone else is better suited to answering questions then, they can refer you to that person. Make it clear that you want to get direct information and will be happy to hear any information they have to share.

Most prospective interviewees are willing to spare twenty to thirty minutes to respond to your question. They may be ready to talk on phone or meet you in their workplace. If you are given a choice between the two, choose to have the interview in the workplace. This will enable you to learn more and make a stronger connection with them.

The Phases

Before the Interview

You should call the person the day before the interview to confirm the appointment. If you are not sure where the interviewee's office is located you can ask at this time. Plan to arrive ten minutes before the interview.

Ninety percent of job openings are not advertised. You may learn about job vacancies that are not found in the newspapers or employment offices through such an interview, so prepare yourself so that you make a great impression. Choose clothing that you would wear for a usual job interview.

During the Interview

Take a pen and notebook: Pretend to be a reporter. It is not necessary to write down everything. However, there might be some phone numbers, names, and other information that you will want to remember.

Take a copy of your resume: Find out what qualities and qualifications the employers look for while hiring. If the situation is appropriate, you can ask the interviewee to review your resume.

Introduce yourself: Once you arrive, you will typically be met by a front desk employee who will introduce you to the interviewee. When you meet him, thank him for taking the time to speak with you. Once again make it clear that you want to learn more about the person's particular career field. Adopt an informal style of conversation during the course of the informational interview.

Be courteous and professional: Maintain good posture and eye contact. Make positive remarks and be light hearted but professional.

Show interest and be enthusiastic: Talk in an informal way and show interest. Ask concise and direct questions. You can refer to the list you have prepared to keep track of your questions but do not curb spontaneous discussion.

Share some things about yourself: You may share some facts related to yourself, but remember that your main purpose is to gather information and learn as much as possible about the field in preparation for a future career.

Many times, the informational interviews turn into employment interviews. If this happens, verify that there is a job opening and emphasize your skills and how they are related to the particular job.

Do not ask for a job: You should not ask for any job during an informational interview. Employers agree to such an interview only because they are sure that it will not be used as an opportunity to seek a job.

If, in the course of the interview, you determine that it is a good job for you, wait until the next day to speak to the employer. The next, call the employer, tell him that the interview helped to confirm your interest in that career, and you wish to formally apply for a position.

The interviewee might offer you a job or an internship. There are many instances where employers have offered jobs to the people who have conducted such interviews. If it is a good offer, go ahead and accept it.

If you ask only for information, you will be treated differently than people who are only interested in a job. Approach the employer by seeking job advice rather than an actual job.

Stay on the right track: Do not waste time asking unnecessary questions.

Listen to them: Listening is a very important part of communication. In addition to asking questions, you should listen carefully. Show them that what they are saying is important to you.

Expand your network of contacts: This interview is like an investment. You spend time with the interviewee sharing information about yourself, asking questions, and getting advice. You are investing your time with him in the hope of gaining something. By spending time with you, he is also hoping to gain something. It is a good idea to keep in touch with each other after the interview ends so that you can both continue to benefit from each other.

Even if the interviewee does not offer you a job, he may be able to refer you to other employers.

Ask for referrals: Before leaving, remember to ask the interviewee if he knows other people who might be willing to speak to you. Ask permission to use his name when contacting potential interviewees.

After the Interview

Thank people: Make sure that you send a letter or card within three days to thank the interviewees. This will help to stay in touch with them. Them that talking to them has been very helpful and that you are grateful to them for taking time out of their day to meet with you. To add a personal touch, you can include a quote they said during the interview. You may also want to ask them to send any information that they think would be helpful for your career. Include your phone number and address at the end.

Record, analyze, and evaluate: After the interview, remember to write down all of the information that you have gathered. This includes the names of potential future interviewees. Store all of the information together for when you need it. It will be useful for you when you conduct more occupational explorations. Employers are generally impressed by activities like that. It can help pave the way to your ideal job.

When you evaluate the interview, you should ask yourself:

- What is it that you have learned from the interview (consider both the negatives and positives)?

- Does this information that I have gathered match with my interests, values, goals, and abilities?

- What is it that I still have to find out?

- What should my action plan be?

Conclusion

Asking questions can help you to learn about unpublished job opportunities. Even if you do not adopt some formal procedure, just chatting with people on the bus or while waiting in line can lead you to unknown job opportunities.

Questions Asked in Informational Interviews

Here is a list of questions that can be asked during informational interviews:

1. How did you become interested in this particular field?

2. What led you to your current job?

3. How do the knowledge and skills you learned in college apply to this job?

4. Describe your typical day in this job.

5. What future trends do you see for this particular career field?

6. What is your most satisfying accomplishment in this job?

7. What do employers look for in candidates who apply for a job in this field?

8. What is it that you like the most or least about this job?

9. What can I do now to prepare myself for a similar job after I graduate?

10. What advice would you like to give to college students who are interested in this

career field?

11. What are the things you learned about this work that you did not know when you graduated?

12. What job search techniques would you suggest for those who have recently graduated?

13. What should I look for in a boss when applying for jobs?

14. What is the "typical" path of this career field?

15. How do employers in this field feel about employees who have a liberal arts degree?

16. Does your organization participate in any internship programs? Can you tell me about them?

17. What are training experiences, trade journals, or professional associations that may help new professionals in this career field?

18. Could I use you as a contact when I start looking for a job or an internship?

Chapter 9: The Power of Storytelling

Storytelling is the ability to tell a story in a way that the listener feels they relate and understand. Anyone can tell a story, but it takes a special type of storytelling for the listener to be able to actually feel what is happening. When you are in a job interview, and the interviewer asks you to tell them about a time something happened, they want you to tell them a story about your past. If your story is uninteresting and not personalized, it is not going to be something that stands out to them. However, if you have a story that they can relate to, and they feel connected to, it could possibly be something that they remember you by and it could even be something that lands you the job.

How can you use this strong tool in your interviews? You can use storytelling when you are answering any long question that requires you to give an example of a time you did something in the past. Examples of these questions are:

- Tell me about a time when you faced a

challenge at work, and how you got through it.

- Tell me about a time a decision was made at work and you disagreed with it. How did you handle this situation?

- Tell me your greatest professional strengths and how you have used it in your past employment.

- Tell me about a time when you saw a problem at work and explain how you solved it.

- Tell me about a time when you made a mistake at work and how it was resolved.

- Give me an example of a time when you worked on a team and what helped you accomplish.

These are all questions that are commonly asked in interviews that could benefit from being told an answer in a story format. To do this, you will need some skills in storytelling in the context of an interview. We will look into these skills now.

The first thing that you need to do when telling a story related to an interview question is to remember that the interviewer is looking for the answer. The story can help them to relate to you in a personal way and to see how you have had to deal with struggles in the past, but they want to know the answer to the question. For this, you should always start with the answer. Start with one sentence that completely answers the question. As an example, if you are telling them about a time when you faced a challenge at work and how you got through it, begin by saying that you once had all your staff called in sick on the same day, and you solved the problem by creatively moving staff around in the office to make sure that all of the important tasks got done before the ones that could wait. After you insert with a one-sentence solution, then you can start to tell the details. The details are still helpful, but you want to start with the actual answer so that the interviewer hears it right away and that they know you are responding to exactly what they are asking. Answering the question in the first sentence also shows you are confident in your answer and that you knew what to say right away.

After you answer the question, you can start to provide the background information. The interviewer will likely be interested in this information because they want to know exactly how you accomplished solving your problem. They will want to know all of the details so that they can tell what you are capable of. You can provide the context of why the challenge occurred and why you were the one that had to solve it. Any related information will be interesting and helpful to the interviewer who is listening to your story.

After you provide the context, explain why you were the one that had to deal with the challenge. You'll want to explain your role in the process, talk about how you were the one to solve it, and why it was not the responsibility of everyone else. It can also make you seem like someone who sees problems and fixes them. The way that you word this part of the story is important because it will reflect who you are considered by the interviewer. The interviewer will more than likely love to see you as a leader or someone who sees problems and fixes them. They may not, however, love to see you as the person who made a mistake. For this, it is important how you word this part of the story. You want the story to show all of the good attributes that you have. This is another reason why it is helpful to plan the story out in advance. If you go through the story in advance, you can define your role as something that the employer actually wants to see.

After you define your role, you will want to share the results of the story. This is when you tell how the problem worked out. You can tell if your problem solving worked or if you had to figure out something else afterwards. You do want to keep this step in mind when you are choosing your story that you would like to tell. This is because you want the story to have positive results when you tell it to the person who is interviewing you. You do not want them to see you as a person who failed or someone who does not have the results. Stories of failed results are not stories that should be told in interviews unless they're asked for. For this, you also want to keep this part of the storytelling in mind when you are choosing a story because you want your role to be a positive one. You want your role to portray who you can be, and that is the perfect employee for the opening that the employer currently has.

After you finish telling your story, consider taking some time to make sure that the lesson of your story is clear. You do not want to tell the story in an interview that does not have a purpose or point. You do not want to tell the story that has nothing to do with the question asked. If you think your story only slightly relates to the question, or that its relation was not clear, it is your job to make sure that the lesson of the story is shown clearly by the end of your speech. You can't simply state what the lesson is, or you can use an example to show it to your interviewer. You do not want the interviewer to get the wrong impression; you want them to see the side of you that you were trying to portray. After all, you did just tell an entire story to show why you would be a good fit for a job. Do you want the story to be worth it and come across the way you actually intend?

Let's look at an example. Think about a person who has interviewed you and asked you the question, "Tell me about a time you made a mistake at work, and how you recovered from it." To answer this question in a story format, you could write something like:

"One time, I gave the wrong order to a customer, and I had to fix this problem before the reputation of the business was ruined. When I was 16, I worked in a little old grocery store in the middle of my small town. This grocery store was one of the few establishments in a few miles' radius, so it had multiple different functions. One of the things the grocery store had was a deli counter. Behind the deli counter, was a broiler. This meant that people who came into the grocery store wanted to get fresh broiled chicken. My job, as a teenager, was to cook this chicken.

One day, I got a call that a customer wanted one dozen chicken legs. This was our first order of the day, so I knew we had plenty of chicken. The customer would come in two hours later, so I figured I would just cook the chicken in an hour and a half so it would be hot and ready when they arrived to pick it up. However, when I went over to cook the chicken a half hour before the customer was going to arrive, I found out that there were only 11 chicken legs thawed and ready to cook. This was a big problem. I told the customer that I would have 12 chicken legs ready for them, and I could only have 11. To handle this, I put the 11 chicken legs in the broiler along with a few extra pieces of different parts of the chicken. I then went right to the phone.

Once I got to the phone, I called the customer who ordered the 12 chicken legs. I called them to explain the problem and to offer any solutions that may help. I gave the customer three choices. I told them that they could either wait an extra hour for another chicken leg to unthaw, that they could have a discount on their 11 chicken legs, or that they could have some other pieces of meat along with their chicken legs to make up for the missing piece.

I could have just ignored this and given the customer the eleven chicken legs, hoping that they did not notice that one was missing. This would have been bad customer service, and it would have given the grocery store a bad reputation. It would have affected my job, as I'm sure my boss would have heard of it. It would have affected my guilt level as well because I would have felt bad about not giving the customer what they wanted and what they paid for.

It was not easy to call the customer. It was actually difficult. I had to tell them that I messed up and I did not have what they wanted. However, they appreciated my customer service. They appreciated that I called and told them the truth that I had made a mistake and that I wanted to fix it. They chose one of my three options and happily picked up the chicken. They never complained of the situation, so they must not have been too upset.

The moral of the story is I did not carefully check we had enough chicken before telling the customer that I could give it to them. However, I did help solve the problem in the right way. The story shows me that honesty is always the best policy. Even when I make mistakes, I always need to own up to them to fix them. I learned this at the young age of 16, and I have been perfecting my morals and work ever since."

Looking at this example, it started by telling the answer to the question. It then gave the context and some background information, explained the mistake and finished by sharing the results and making the lesson clear.

Telling stories can be a strong tool in interviews, especially when the interviewer is asking to hear one. Make sure that you have your stories ready in advance so that you can tell the ones that portray your best sides when you are actually in the interview. Make sure to follow the five steps when telling the story so that you can tell it in a way that stands out and shows them everything that you want them to see. If you follow these tips and tricks while telling stories in your interviews, your interviewer will see more into your personality through them, and your stories will show what you are truly capable of. This will make your stories a great addition to your interview skills and help you land your dream job.

Now that we have looked into all of the ways that words and verbal communication can help you and your interviews, let's look into how your nonverbal communication can help you as well.

Chapter 10: Emotional Intelligence in your Job Interview.

First of all, you cannot understand the functioning of the whole world, without understanding yourself. Using emotional intelligence is the first step to be able to look critically at the people around us. Social competences, such as empathy, assertiveness, confidence, cooperation, are essential aspects of your personal life. It depends on it whether we will be the soul of the party, liked, and accepted. We will not achieve this only due to high IQ or scientific knowledge.

It is also worth realizing that during the interview, it is our qualities such as the ability to behave appropriately, the ease of establishing interpersonal relationships, understanding the situation, the skill of persuasion makes up the first impression and can determine whether the employer will see us as a future employee.

Communication Skills at Job Interviews

You have come too far to mess things up. You have done a lot of research, spent your time to gather all that you need for the interview, and even groomed yourself for the occasion. It would be a pity to lose it all for mistakes you did on the actual interview. Remember the objective of your interview is to land a job offer. To realize this objective, you will, by all means, have to prove that you are the best there is. If you are waiting to do big things to blow away your hiring managers, it is time to wake up and smell the coffee. It is the little things that matter and that will possibly work for you or against you.

What to do during the interview

Say Hi to the receptionist

It is common courtesy to greet people you meet. You do not have to start up a conversation, as a matter of fact, it is not recommended that you do. If you can, also get his/her name if it is not on a tag somewhere. This is very important since some hiring managers seek to see just how keen you are and aware of your environment or even friendliness by asking you the name of the receptionist or even the guard at the door.

Which might seem harsh but valid. Hiring managers do not want to hire robots or persons who say they are friendly and do not care enough to know the name of the receptionist or even the guard.

Have the right body language

Your body language will communicate just as much as the information you offer to your hiring managers. You do not want to be in a situation that you say you are confident but your body language reeks of lacking in confidence. Try as much as you can to have your body language convey the same message as your words. If you say you are confident, do maintain an upright posture, maintain eye contact and have a convincing tone.

If slouching, fidgeting and looking down are bad habits that you possess, you can get rid of them by practicing in front of a mirror. Pull up a chair and observe your body language.

Also, avoid flattering behaviors like biting your lower lip or winking. You might be unaware that you wink at people or it is just something you picked up over the years, regardless, you might have to actively subdue them.

Have the right tone of voice

Like your body language, your tone will also speak a thousand words. You could repeat that you know how to do your job a thousand times but if you do not sound like you can, your words are worth nothing. Have a tone that will inspire confidence in your hiring manager.

So, how does one sound more confident during a job interview?

Take your time to think over the question, gather your thoughts before you answer. The recommended time to take for this is five seconds. Now it might seem like such a long time and awkwardness might set in but the interviewer sees it as you giving your answer some consideration.

Always have an interested tone though factual and straight forward. You should keep away from rising your pitch towards the end of your statements as this will turn them into questions making you seem uncertain of what you are saying. You should however vary your tone depending on the question and what it relates to. Do not overdo it though.

Do not apologize for being nervous. Doing this will actually put more scrutiny on just how worried you are about your performance.

Use a firm handshake

There are individuals who are sucker for firm handshakes. There are those who can tell who you are from the way you shake their hand. Just ensure you do not hurt your hiring manager while you are at it.

Sit only when you are asked to

When you walk into the room, only take a seat when they ask you to and not before. It is a sign of politeness. It is the same thing as when someone is at your door. They should wait until you invite them in (especially if you are not as close).

Have your loose items on the floor right next to you

You should never place your items on the interviewer desk unless they say that it is okay that you do so. Have all these items placed comfortably on your lap or on a coffee table right in front of you. As for your briefcase, have it right at your feet or on your side.

Have your mobile turned off

You do not want to have disruptions during the interview. Setting your phone to vibrate just won't cut it.

Thank your interviewer

The fact that they choose you out of the hundreds and thousands of applicants is worth saying thank you.

What not to do during an interview

Do not assume the interview is done until you are out of the door

From the moment you walk in the office the interview is on. Everything from your behavior, use of words to attitude is under scrutiny. As such, you should be overly careful of what you say. After all, everything you say and do will be held and used against you. Be at the very top of our game until you walk out that door, or better yet, out of the company building. You never know who you will bump into on your way out so be respectful to everyone.

Do not be too relaxed

Sure, the interview is a platform for you to gauge is you will love the job and you are encouraged to be relaxed. You should however not treat your hiring manager like your long lost friend (even if he/she is). You should be friendly, but remember you are seeking to be impressive. Being too relaxed may have you slipping up and saying the wrong things altogether.

Never badmouth your old job

Maybe your former boss was the devil incarnate and is probably the reason why you left your previous job. But be it as it may, you should not point it out to your hiring manager. As far as your hiring company is concerned, you should get along with everyone you are given to work with no matter how difficult they are. So rather than badmouth your previous boss or company, speak of the achievements you made as a team. Doing this will also keep you from coming across as self-centered.

Do not freak out if you do not know the answer

Some hiring managers are known for putting their interviewees on the spot. And since you never know what kind of hiring manager you will get, you should always be prepared. Never freak out when you are presented with a question that you do not know the answer to. Freaking out will make you lose all sense of rationality making things even worse. So how should you hand yourself in such a situation?

First, and most important, you should calm down. Freaking out will rise your heart beat rate, rise your temperature and cloud your judgments. Be sure to take deep breaths and convince yourself that all is well. After all, it is okay not to know the answer to a question.

Second, even when you do not know the answer to the question provided, never say that you do not know the answer without giving it a try. Also, as you try to give your answer, do not make things up. Hiring managers are not stupid and will be sure to see right through the crap.

You also have the option of asking follow up questions to ensure you understand the question right. Ask for clarification and more details that will help you provide a better answer.

But even after the clarification, if the question still proves difficult to answer, be sure to iterate what you do know rather than what you do not know. Also, you should spell out the steps that you could take to get to the answer of the question presented. This way, even while you may not have the answer at the moment, you assure the hiring managers that you have the ability to get to the answer if afforded more time.

Never lie

You should, by all means, be straight forward with your hiring manager. It is as they say, the truth always has a way of coming out. When lying, you may not be able to hold a sincere flowing conversation with the hiring manager and this might be a major turn off. Truth be told, honesty is the best policy. Even when you land that job position you will have started on the wrong foot and it is only a matter of time before your lies catch up with you.

Chapter 11: Can You Coach Others?

Interview Question

What have you done to help a peer understand skill areas to strengthen? Give an example.

Why do they ask this question?

Bad Answer

An example of a bad answer to this question would be:

I once had a group member in school who struggled to understand the basic accounting concepts in our accounting class. I knew the person was going to take some time to understand the concepts, so I just ended up doing their work for them so that we could finish the project in a timely manner.

Taking over for the group member helped us get a good grade.

Why this is a bad answer:
Even though you show that your group member has room for development, you don't really show the steps you took to develop them. You don't show that

you were interested in developing them. For this question, you have to show willingness to understand another person's weaknesses, and the desire to help them.

Good Answer

An example of a good answer to this question would be:

I once had a classmate in my tax research class ask me how to get better at tax research. I helped them understand what skills and knowledge to strengthen by asking them a series of questions. I asked them if they knew hierarchy of authority in tax research, and I also asked them where they started once they received a research topic. By understanding the person's approach and current knowledge, I was able to develop a plan for them to improve their skills.

Good Answer

An example of a good answer to this question would be:

I once had a group member who had a really bad attitude during a group project, so I took the person aside and spoke to them. I told them that they seemed disinterested in the work, and I asked if there was something bothering them.

It turns out that there was something bothering them. They had just failed a project in another class and that is what was affecting them. The group member apologized to me because they weren't aware that they were coming off as disinterested. In this case I was able to provide the feedback in an appropriate manner without embarrassing or offending my group member.

Why this is a good answer:
This is a good answer because it shows how you provided feedback in a tasteful and appropriate manner. You took the person aside and had a personal conversation. You also were not harsh to the person's face.

Interview Question

Give me an example of feedback received and how you put the information to use.

Why do they ask this question?

Are you able to receive feedback without taking it personally?

Can you take feedback and improve on it, or does it go in one ear and out the other?

Bad Answer

An example of a bad answer to this question would be:

One of my prior bosses told me that I was too ambitious and that I didn't need to work so hard. I hear that a lot actually --- that I work too hard.

Why this is a bad answer:
Don't say this in an interview. This is a very typical answer. Nobody like someone that tries to show off by saying that their biggest weakness is working too hard. Just think of a couple of examples where you've received constructive feedback and use those. Do not say your one weakness is that you work too hard or care too much though.

Good Answer

An example of a good answer to this question would be:
After a project in school that involved public speaking, I received some feedback from the professor that I was monotoned and slumped over. It was hard for me to take the feedback at first, but

I knew that improving my public speaking is key to my success in business. I took the professor's advice, and I also started attending toastmasters to improve my public speaking. After taking the feedback and analyzing it, I performed very well on my next public speaking project I had in school.

Why this is a good answer:

This is a good answer because it highlights not only your ability to take feedback but to also improve on that feedback. This candidate not only received the feedback from the professor, but they also improved their performance in the future by taking the professors feedback positively.

Chapter 12: Master Your Phone Interview

Being interviewed over the phone is a unique and challenging experience. In a limited amount of time, you have to be prepared to sell your appropriateness for the opportunity in order to secure a spot in the next round of interviews. In order to succeed, you will need to understand the different types of phone interviews you may encounter, how to respond most appropriately to the questions asked and what to do in order to gain clarity for the next steps in the process.

So, what is a phone interview? Of course, it is an interview that takes place over the phone but there are a few permutations of the phone interview to prepare for. Sometimes, you may not even realize that you are being interviewed.

The role of the person on the phone is often that of recruiter. The first type of phone interview is not really an interview at all: a recruiter contacting you with the intention of setting up an-in person interview. The recruiter would like to confirm your interest in the position and provide you with the details of when your interview will take place and who you will be meeting with. The recruiter has every intention of setting up an interview for you at this point unless you give her a reason to be concerned.

There could be variety of reasons that the phone call is eliciting concern on the recruiter's behalf such as:

- You answered the call in an unprofessional manner and seem confused as to why you are receiving a phone call. You may not be expecting a call and you are treating the recruiter like a telemarketer until you figure out what the call is concerning.

- You seem uninterested in interviewing for the position.

- You are asking several basic questions about the job, demonstrating that you do not remember much of anything about the company or the role.

- You do not sound professional on the phone. Perhaps you are too focused on the salary or the hours for the position or you are being too candid or lax in your language.

- You cannot be heard or understood. You may be in an area with bad cell phone reception or trying to whisper at your current place or employment or your kids are trying to talk over you when you are on the phone.

As a recent college graduate several years ago, I attempted to answer a call in Times Square from a recruiter representing a large media company. Needless to say, one of the busiest places in the world was (and is) one of the loudest as well. After a few responses of "Can you repeat that?" the opportunity was lost. I was told by the recruiter that he would call me back but that never happened.

- You are inflexible in your availability to come in for an interview. The recruiter may have proposed several times for you to attend an in-person interview but none of those times work for you due to your work schedule or other commitments.

While the recruiter may have called you with every intention of setting up an interview, a point or two of concern may have eliminated your chances. You will be told that you will be contacted once the company has made a decision rather than being called in for an interview.

In some cases, the recruiter attempted to reach you but was unsuccessful in doing so or experienced an area of concern that eliminated that possibility. That may include:

- An unprofessional voicemail message. Your first verbal impression might be your voicemail message so make sure that it is professionally appropriate. Provide a message that clearly states your name that you are sorry that you missed the call and that you will return the call as soon as time allows. Avoid any voicemails messages that include extended words of inspiration, attempts at demonstrating your vocal or rap talents or allowing your kids to record a cute message on your behalf.

- A voicemail message that is not in English or you do not state your name. The recruiter has to know that she reached you. Always provide your name in your message and if you expect that many of the callers to your phone are non-English speakers, provide at least a message in your language of preference as well as one in English.

- Your phone is out of order. Whether it is a permanent change in number or you have used up your prepaid minutes, an out of service phone will lead to a missed opportunity. Unless you possess unique skills that are unlikely to be found in other candidates (and even then), a recruiter is not going to chase you down to find you on social media or email.

- Someone answering the phone who does not take a message for you with all of the necessary details.

So, how can you ensure a smooth phone screening and no stumbling blocks to the in-person interview?

- If you do not recognize the phone number, assume that it may be a recruiter. Answer the call with your name and in a professional manner.

- Be prepared to talk when you answer the phone. If you are unprepared to talk, let the phone go to voicemail.

- If you are prepared to talk but you see that your cell phone reception is very weak or your train is about to go underground, let the call go to voicemail.

- If you planned to be able to talk but something came up unexpectedly, take the recruiter's name and number, and ask when you may call back.

- When you are job seeking, you should have a general idea of your schedule of availability so that setting up an in-person interview is not an arduous process.

- It would be difficult to access every application you have made over the last few months in order to be prepared every time the phone rings but it would be helpful to maintain a basic list that you can quickly peruse for information to refresh your memory once you are contacted.

- If you absolutely have to, fake it until you make it. Make it clear that you are interested in the opportunity when speaking on the phone until you have a reason not to be interested. Do your best to show enthusiasm while you are trying to figure things out.

By following the suggestions above, you will be able to avoid the pitfalls of the seemingly "simple" process of setting up the interview when the recruiter calls you.

All conditions being perfect, it is best to answer the call then and there but sometimes it is not the ideal time. It may be difficult to reach the recruiter later but it is better than to pick up the phone in a bad reception zone or a noisy area.

The next style of phone interview is a pre-screening, which involves being asked a handful of questions to determine if you match the basic criteria needed for the role. The recruiter is trying to avoid having to meet in-person with candidates who are clearly not a fit for the job.

One of the challenges of this type of phone interview is that you may or may not be given a warning in advance. Some recruiters may email you to set up a time for a brief phone screening whereas others will just launch into their questions. What this means is that you must always be prepared. These brief few minutes are your opportunity to sell yourself for the role. The recruiter will not give much consideration to whatever was going on at the time of the call that may have been a distraction to you or hurt your chances of putting your best foot forward.

While you cannot anticipate all of the questions that may be asked, the questions do tend to veer to the basics during a phone screen. A recruiter will generally not have an expert knowledge of the position that you are interviewing for. He will be looking for a basic skills match and looking to weed out people with major question marks in their backgrounds.

The key here is that time is limited. The recruiter is trying to determine your basic fit for the role. Similar questions may be asked by the same person during an in person interview, which you can answer with greater depth and detail at that time.

No matter what questions are asked, consider the following:

How can I demonstrate that I am a great fit for this role when I answer this question? An interview isn't about you but an opportunity to show why you are a great fit for the job.

Without having the opportunity to see someone in person, there is a connection that is lost over the phone. Try to project a good level of energy and enthusiasm over the phone. If normally you are subdued and a quiet talker, you may need to push yourself outside of your comfort zone for the phone interview. In order to project your voice and maintain your enthusiasm, you may want to stand up for the phone interview and speak a bit louder than you normally would. Although it might be tempting, avoid pacing around. Your phone might hit certain bad reception areas if you are walking around so avoid having the phone cut in and out.

If you are given the opportunity to prepare for the phone screening, there are several steps that you can take to put your best foot forward:

Research: When you know that you have a phone screening to prepare for, don't be reliant upon remembering what you learned about the company when you submitted your resume. Look up the company website and read current articles about the organization.

Review: Reread the job description for the position (you saved it, right? If not, a Google search might help you to find the old posting), the cover letter that you sent as well as your resume.

Consider: What questions you might be asked about your background and determine how you can explain any bumps in your career journey- such as an inconsistent work history or if you have ever been fired.

If you need to, admit to any mistakes or errors in judgment but focus on what you have learned as well. Try to stay light on the negativity and focus on the positive.

Space: Find a quiet area where you will be taking the call. If you are at home, make sure that your family knows that you have an important call at that time and you will let them know when you are off of the phone.

Do not ask about the salary over the phone. Just like it is not appropriate to ask about the salary during your first in person interview, it is not appropriate to ask here either.

The recruiter might ask what salary you are seeking as a way to weed out candidates over the phone. Provide a wide salary range as opposed to a number. Once you have responded, you can inquire as to what range the company has in mind.

When you are asked if you have any questions, don't focus on the hours of the job or the fringe benefits. Use this as your opportunity to gain clarity on the next steps in the process as well as the recruiter's contact information.

Ask what are the next steps in the process and when you can expect to hear back. This will provide you with a timeline for your follow up strategy. If you are told that you will hear back within two weeks, it would be acceptable for you to contact the recruiter again somewhere in the range of two and a half to three weeks later.

Make sure to get the recruiter's full name and email address. Email the recruiter a thank you note within one day of your phone interview. Avoid a generic note that can be used for anyone at any time. Include a couple of specific details that were discussed and a reference as to your strong qualifications.

"Dear Ms. Thomas,

Thank you for taking the time over the phone to discuss the position of Systems Analyst. I enjoyed learning more about the organization's planned expansion into the South American market. Given my knowledge of the region and relevant experience in the areas of banking and finance, I am excited to learn more. I am looking forward to the next steps in the process.

Regards"

The third, and final, type of phone interview is not a pre-screening but your actual "first interview". The most common reason that the first interview takes place over the phone is for logistical purposes: candidates from outside of the geographic area are being considered for the position and to be respectful of everyone's time, the phone interview is replacing the need to travel to an in-person interview. This style of interview is becoming less commonplace as interviews with remote candidates are more commonly being conducted over Skype or similar web based application.

Being able to participate in a formal interview over the phone does have some advantages for the applicant. As you cannot be seen by the interviewer, you can keep your notes in front of you. This might include a list of the questions that you want to ask, reminders of particular accomplishments that you want to be sure to mention and possibly even your resume.

If there is more than one person on the other end of the line, you have to pay special attention as to when it is your time to talk. The first interviewer may have just finished talking and you are ready to respond but the second interviewer has something to say. When there is more than one interviewer, allow a brief moment before you respond to each question before you respond.

As opposed to a briefer pre-screening interview, you should provide answers that go more in-depth and paint a picture of your strong qualifications for the job.

Chapter 13: Reviewing
The Interview

You've articulated your strengths, you've learned to tell your story, and you've practiced to become your very best. Now what?

Even though you've gotten much better at interviewing by learning how to communicate your story, you probably won't deliver a knockout performance in every interview. The truth is that there is always room to get better, and there is one thing in particular you can do to get even better at interviewing. Evaluate how the interview went and think about your perceptions of the organization *before* they give you a job offer.

Why bother thinking about something that just happened?

People have a tendency to believe that any given outcome was inevitable once it has happened, even if they didn't know what the outcome would be before it happened. If you wait until you hear that an organization is not interested in hiring you, you may think that you knew this was going to happen all along. When you think back on the interview after having been turned down, it will inevitably seem like it went poorly. You may blame yourself, the interviewer (perhaps they didn't ask you the right questions), or someone else (perhaps there are many overqualified job seekers in your area, and they're taking all the entry-level jobs that should be given to younger people). Your memories will have faded and you'll think back on only the negative aspects of the interview.

Alternatively, what if you're offered the job? It's tempting to believe that this means that your interviewing skills are absolutely amazing and you couldn't have done any better. You might feel that you don't even need to practice the next time you decide to look for a job. After all, you're a master, and getting future jobs will be as easy as showing up to interview on the scheduled day. (We hope you can read our sarcasm.)

Putting an interview experience out of mind as soon as you walk out the door can also lead you to make the wrong decision about accepting the job. If you're presented with a strong job offer, you may find yourself deciding that you really like the organization. Perhaps the hiring manager said a lot of great things about you when they called with the offer; maybe they talked up all of the benefits you would receive if you worked there. If you have received an offer without already deciding whether the organization is right for you, it will be really difficult to objectively evaluate their offer. That decision is too important to let someone make for you.

And if you're still not convinced that you need to reflect on your job interview, do it for another reason. If nothing else, writing down the questions that you answered well, or the questions that you didn't address particularly well, gives you great content for a thank you letter.

For all of these reasons, it's best to evaluate the interview experience before you learn its outcome. It is very important to *write down* your perceptions so you don't forget them later. With written notes, you'll have an objective impression of how the interview went that you can then use to improve your interview skills in the future as well as to decide whether you want to accept a job offer.

How to Reflect on Your Interview Experience

As soon as you have a moment to yourself after the interview is over, think about your overall impressions.

Then think about the interview in chronological order, stopping at each memorable event (walking into the office, shaking hands, greeting your interviewer, and so forth) and again at each interview question that you can remember. Evaluate each of these in your mind and then compose written notes.

After thinking about the interview by yourself, talk about the experience with several people. Ideally, these should be people who will ask you a lot of questions. Conversation will help you to reflect on things that may have escaped your attention. For instance, a friend might ask if people were smiling in the office. If you talk about this on the same day that you had the interview, you'll be able to remember whether you saw people who seemed to be happy to be at their jobs. If you try to remember this next month when you're evaluating the job offer, your recollection won't be as accurate.

Next, jot down what you learned about the company. What are the expectations that were communicated to you? What did you learn about the company culture? Were they asking questions that focused on specific tasks or skills? If so, these will probably be key to your success on the job.

Finally, think through the highlights, lowlights, and what you plan to do in future interviews. To help you along in this process of evaluating your interview, we've created an Interview Evaluation Guide.

Interview Evaluation Guide

<u>**Overview**</u>

- **How well prepared did you feel walking into the interview?**
- <u>Which questions surprised you or caught you off guard?</u>

<u>**The positives**</u>

- Which of your answers best communicated your story? What worked about those answers?

The negatives

- Which of your answers did not communicate your story very well? Why did they fall short? (Perhaps your answer didn't fit with the rest of your story or was confusing. Maybe you just couldn't think of an answer.)

The company

- **Did you get a clear sense of what you would do on a daily basis?**
- Do you know who you would work with? Who would you report to? Who would you interact with on a daily basis? Who would you interact with only occasionally?
- Do you think you could get along reasonably well with the people you met? (Include everyone you interacted with, not just the interviewers.)
- Do you think this position will allow you to use your skills and knowledge and help you meet your career goals?
- Do you know what will be expected of you, how you will be evaluated, and what you will need to do to excel in this

position?

- <u>Are you excited about the possibility of working for this organization and with these people?</u>

For the future

What might you do differently during your next interview?

Disliking an organization

If you don't like to fail, you may find yourself writing something like, "I don't think I liked this organization." That way, you'll be able to soothe your ego if they don't extend you an offer. You'll just say to yourself, *that job would have been awful—I'm glad they didn't bother calling me back!*

It's fine to write down negative opinions if they are in fact true. But try to avoid being pre-emptively negative in order to save your feelings. This is a little like breaking up with someone just so they don't break up with you first. Why not give it a little time? It's okay to like a job or an organization even if you're not exactly the right fit, right now. That doesn't mean you'll never get to work there. In fact, a better position may open up in the future, or your future work experiences may make you a more desirable candidate.

If you evaluate an organization negatively just to feel better about rejection in the future, you'll also be less likely to be happy or satisfied with the job offer when it does come. You'll look back at your written reflections and think, *oh, but I didn't like this organization. Maybe I shouldn't accept the offer*.

If you're always evaluating jobs or organizations negatively and you know that it's not because you're afraid of rejection, you may be applying to the wrong jobs. In this case, it's time to do more research about organizations before you bother applying and going on interviews and to honestly evaluate whether this is indeed the field you want to work in. For instance, if you find yourself frustrated that every banking job in New York City requires ridiculous hours, perhaps you need to consider living in a different area or working for a less prestigious firm where the expectations may be a little lower.

Success is Not Measured in Job Offers

You should always remember that whether or not you get a job offer shouldn't define how well the interview went. You can make a great impression in the mind of an interviewer and still not be the best fit for the job. If you are considering a job offer and reflecting on the interview, keep in mind that the cost of a bad fit is high for both you and your employer. If you don't think you can deliver what the job requires, it may be best for you to pass on the offer. And instead of thinking about whether you aced an interview, instead of letting the outcome dictate how you feel about the process, you can define for yourself whether or not the interview was a success. If you can remember this while you're in the interview itself, it will help you be more objective and less nervous. It will also help you to stay positive throughout the whole job search process.

Chapter 14: Dealing with Realities

A well thought out job search that focuses on the right fit starts with some definitions.

- What industry or industry segments do you want to work in?
- Do you want to work in an established company or one new to the industry?
- Where would you most like to work or where else would you be willing to accept a relevant job geographically?
- Given your present circumstances, how much of a risk-taker are you?

Clearly, your perception of yourself, and how you are convinced that others see you, helps you rebrand yourself. Positive results that are relevant to the needs of your target company, and presented credibly, are what will get you in the door and give you the opportunity to excel. But to get there, you have to deal with realities: besides company financial status, try to measure the quality and staying power of the management.

You should understand the status of products and services, morale factors affecting productivity or turnover, and the gaps and pains the company needs to resolve to improve its competitiveness and profitability. The level of your success depends heavily on how well your experience and results can help close the gaps and manage the pain.

Before you get too far into your decision making, make sure to check your priorities and share your thoughts with the people who most matter in your life.

Where do you start?

Unless you're single and responsible only for yourself, your first reality check is your family. If you're married, start obviously with your spouse. Hopefully, there are no surprises. If you've been out of work, your spouse is well aware that you need to produce income and also well aware of what kind of situation can restore your confidence, make you happiest and probably most successful.

If an important new job requires a move, then what? One of your many considerations may be spouse employment.

Do you go alone for a while until you're sure things will work the way you envisioned while your spouse continues to work and maybe starts his/her own job search? What about children? Do you have kids in school? If they're very young, they're probably also very malleable. They can move and make new friends in days and this can turn out to be wonderful adventure for them. If they're older, not so easy. It depends on what grades they're in school, what outside activities and, maybe more than anything else, what close friendships they may have to leave behind.

The importance of family support

Your family is your main source of support. If you really like the new opportunity, you may need to sell a lot to get them onboard. Selling in this case is to illustrate benefits to them, dealing first with emotions like fear, anger and insecurity, especially over losing friends and facing the changes inherent in a strange new place. While they may resist and experience some temporary setback, you need to first overcome the emotions and then convince them that this new situation is good for them. Not an easy task. But an extension of your role as a salesman.

If you force them to go literally kicking and screaming, or with arms folded across their chests, and given to spurts of anger or crying jags, can you possibly focus enough on your new job to make positive impressions? Maybe you can clear your head and focus during the day, but what about coming home? How much resistance can you put up with and for how long?

Add to that the possibility of leaving behind, or taking with you, elderly or sick parents and the various complications you can imagine.

None of this is meant to scare you or turn you off to what you think could be a great opportunity. It is meant to condition you to the realities, including all of the circumstances you need to be aware of in this life-changing decision.

You want a job with growth potential, where you can excel and maximize your income. Getting to that point is not as simple as finding an ad and acing an interview. It is hard work. Maybe even tedious work. And it takes thoughtful, disciplined research. You never want to make a decision, particularly if it involves a move that can blow up in your face because of factors you didn't know, and, therefore, didn't anticipate. What do you do then? Go back into a job search and possibly move again after your family has gotten settled?

Even if you are fortunate enough to find an opportunity that does not require a move, is it possibly a temporary relief from a problem that could wind up being worse sometime down the line. Make sure to uncover both the good and the bad of the company and its management. Whatever you decide, keeping up the confidence, respect, security and support of your family is fundamental to your success.

Never give up on research

If you can read between the lines and understand where I am going with this, your smartest approach is to invest as much time and effort as possible into meaningful research. And, if you can, find ways for your family to help you. You may be surprised by ideas they come up with and people they may know who can be valuable sources of information. You want to do this right.

Find that situation that lets you excel, where your family, each member, sees something positive. For your spouse, maybe a better job as well, or a better house, better neighborhood, better activities or social circles. For the kids, maybe better schools or camps or colleges than you couldn't have afforded before, along with greater, affordable social opportunities. Maybe a car. You get the picture.

If they are all happy, it is much easier for you to approach that new job with a vigor and excitement that wins you recognition. And it is much easier to come home at night to smiling faces eager to tell you about their new experiences.

My appreciation, and love, of research was instilled in me early in my career by some of the toughest critics I could possibly imagine. They shaped my thinking in ways that have served me well throughout my career. I am grateful to them for whatever successes I have had. And, in retrospect, I've thought many times how glad I am that I was receptive and eager to learn from them. I hope in this book, and particularly in this chapter, that I can pass on some of their wisdom.

As a young journalism student, I had the good fortune of learning from seasoned, street smart newspaper editors who were not impressed by academic writings, but insisted on "clear, correct and concise" articles on any subject. Those words became a mantra. They insisted on the use of correct words, corroboration of facts and background for stories along with absolute adherence to deadlines. I think back sometimes to what I thought were excellent pieces of copy that wound up being slashed and marked up beyond belief. And sometimes even ridiculed.

I once used the word "penultimate" in writing about a tennis player advancing to the semi-finals of a tournament. The loud "you got to be kidding me" response from my instructor obviously has stuck with me as a reminder to express, not impress, with my writing.

An editing assignment a little later on in which a New York Times writer referred to a car "careering" over a curb and into a wall served as another long-time lesson. I confidently changed the word to "careening."

The instructor, who, at night was the editor of The New York Times foreign desk, called me out in class and asked me what "careening" meant and I confidently answered him (to sway to the side).

Then he asked me what "careering" meant and I made an attempt to answer, defending my change and learning a lesson in research when the editor asked me publicly if I had bothered to look up the word or had just chosen to assume I knew more than the writer.

I had mistakenly changed the writer's meaning and imagery. Careering, I learned, meant plunging straight ahead, not swaying to the side. My argument that the word "careering" didn't fit the "clear" part of the mantra fell flat and I learned quickly to make frequent use of both a dictionary and a thesaurus.

A few years later, Journalism degree in my pocket and a graduate of a Defense Department training program, I was an intelligence analyst at the National Security Agency, where research is a challenging and demanding full time business. I collected and analyzed data on a variety of targets, then had to learn to write reports using only precise adjectives and strictly supportable facts. Adjectives like "long" or "short," "big" or "small" or colors like "red" or "blue" or "green" can be interpreted in so many different ways by different people as to be generally meaningless and unsupportable.

The rule of thumb was that each fact had to be proven with input from five different sources and, where possible, was appended with statistical research and photographs. The work was painstaking and exacting, but the sensation of having reports accepted for distribution was exhilarating. With all the bad raps NSA has taken in the past few years, I learned to respect the dedicated professionalism that went into intelligence products. I am still influenced by what I learned there many years ago.

You'll probably never have to write with only absolutely precise adjectives and prove everything you say from five sources, but you will need to learn the discipline of looking at facts through clear eyes, without prejudgment. That will help you analyze and assess industries, companies and people who may influence the rest of your life.

Getting into your "best" company

So, you've identified the industries, the companies and the people you want to pursue. Now what? You want to capitalize on all of the effort you've put into finding industries where you would have the most comfort and expertise and then companies within those industries where the past results of your skills and experience could be most valuable.

Using any sources, including the internet, see if you can find speeches or articles by key executives to get insights into what is going on right now or in the immediate future. With luck, you might find something from an executive in your area of specialization that could be extremely useful in both gaining entry to the company and in interviews.

Don't hesitate to write to someone whose article or speech has impressed you. Look also at press releases to get a better sense of how the company wants to be perceived by its various publics, especially shareholders and customers.

Sift through your notes and drop companies that give you concern. Consider what you're doing as a step towards a long-term relationship. Are you willing to commit long hours, enthusiasm and passion to this organization which may, in fact, consume most of your daily thoughts, not to mention time? Maybe even more than your home life. Are the potential rewards worth the potential risk? As much as possible, make up your mind objectively, with research as your basis.

Don't be talked into a job where there are serious questions. That said, no company, and no job, is perfect. There will always be some level of anxiety. Go back to the earlier thoughts about knowing yourself and make a reasoned decision based on the best intelligence you have been able to muster. Imperfections in a company may be opportunities for you depending on your experience and ability to fix them.

By now, you should have a short list. Maybe even a single company. But, remember, there are no sure things. Hedge a bit. Have alternatives. A Plan "B". Maybe more.

In preparation for your approach to a company, find out what you can about the executives, particularly those who conceivably could influence your future. How old are they? How long have they been with the company? How successful have they been here and in previous organizations? Did they by chance go to the same school or schools that you did? What outside organizations are they involved with?

Most importantly, is there anything in their backgrounds that ties to you? Or to someone you know well? That also could aid your entry into the company. Your very valuable business librarian should be able to steer you to biographical references, by name or by company.

If you can find, or get introduced to, current or former employees of your target companies, ask about these executives. What do these people know or hear about them? Do they have a reputation for fairness and a history of supporting and developing subordinates? Ask their impressions of the company and, while you're at it, check out Glassdoor and similar websites that can provide insights into the company. If you don't know people personally, one of the best ways to find them is through LinkedIn.

Keep moving forward

As in intelligence work, you'll rarely find everything you would like to know. But the more you do find that objectively satisfies your interest, the more your enthusiasm should be piqued. And, presumably, you can find valuable information that can get you in the door and be knowledgeably impressive in interviews. The quality and usefulness of your research should allow you to separate yourself from your competition and give you an opening to prove your worth.

You are now ready to move into the next phase of your strategy: Getting in the door. You might get lucky through your research and establish contact with a key executive, in person, at a business meeting or by phone or letter, or through networking. If you got that person's attention, most likely he/she would contact HR and have them interview you. That's a plus because it moves you to a short list (maybe the top) and requires that the HR people report the results of the meeting to the key executive.

Remember, the comment earlier about being the CEO of You? Well, now you're in charge. Excel in the interview and your chances of landing the job have just soared.

The most likely scenario is that you will need to network into a position which, because of an implied endorsement, may be more powerful than the direct contact. It involves an extra step or two but helps you build relationships for now and the future.

Especially after you have the advantage of learning how to effectively use principles and strategies of networking.

Conclusion

In summary, a job interview is one of the most important meetings in the working life of a person. Interviews serve as a good chance for the employer to assess a prospective new team member, while the candidate assesses their potential bosses. Interview preparation offers candidates the necessary tactics on how to conduct themselves to increase their chances of having a successful interview. Conversely, lack of preparation leads to nervousness and mistakes during the interview process.

As a basic guideline, this book equips a job candidate, whether starting up or experienced candidates, with necessary techniques to ace their next interview process. It offers a step-by-step guide on things one needs to know and do before an interview, things to do during the interview, and things one needs to know and do after the interview. It portrays the significance of reading prior to an interview since it shows candidates how to market themselves to the prospective employers and to be able to assess if the job offer is suitable for them in the process. It also offers insight into the things that should be avoided during an interview. If this guideline is followed, a candidate is assured of ultimate success in their next interview.

CPSIA information can be obtained
at www.ICGtesting.com
Printed in the USA
LVHW010812211120
672146LV00002B/136